STRANGER VIOLENCE

CURRENT ISSUES IN
CRIMINAL JUSTICE
(VOL. 1)

GARLAND REFERENCE LIBRARY
OF SOCIAL SCIENCE
(VOL. 753)

CURRENT ISSUES
IN CRIMINAL JUSTICE

GENERAL EDITORS
Frank P. Williams III
Marilyn D. McShane

STRANGER VIOLENCE
A Theoretical Inquiry

Marc Riedel

GARLAND PUBLISHING, INC. • NEW YORK & LONDON
1993

Library of Congress Cataloging-in-Publication Data

Riedel, Marc.
    Stranger violence : a theoretical inquiry / Marc Riedel.
       p.   cm. — (Current issues in criminal justice ; vol. 1) (Garland reference
library of social science ; vol. 753)
    ISBN 0-8153-0094-8
    1. Crime.   2. Violence.   3. Crime—United States.   4. Violence—United
States.   I. Title.   II. Series.   III. Series: Garland reference library of social
science ; v. 753.
HV6030.R54   1993
364.1'5—dc20   92-432
                                                                                CIP

Printed on acid-free, 250-year-life paper
Manufactured in the United States of America

Series Preface

This work represents the first volume in the Garland Current
Issues in Criminal Justice series. The series is devoted to readable,
scholarly work in criminal justice, particularly work that breaks new
ground or fills in existing gaps in knowledge. Marc Riedel's *Stranger
Violence: A Theoretical Inquiry* fits these purposes admirably. Readers
will find the book to be quite readable, while at the same time
exhibiting a tour-de-force in the area of criminal violence.

Riedel's work adds substantially to the sparse literature on stranger
violence. If he had simply devoted time to exploring the data on this
topic, it would have been enough, but the work goes significantly
beyond an empirical examination of stranger violence. Noting that
one of the major problems in previous criminological work has been
in defining "strangers," Riedel provides a conceptual basis for studying
violence by strangers. He then uses the improved concepts to create a
better understanding of stranger violence. Arguing that stranger
violence is not merely a random phenomenon (after all, an urban area
can be characterized by routine meetings of strangers), Riedel intro-
duces stranger interactions as part of the normal social environment
and distinguishes the forms of interaction, or relationships, that occur.
Based on a combination of settings and relationships, he presents an
intriguing theory of stranger violence. Finally, he relates this theory to
Donald Black's macrotheory of law and explains the effect of stranger
violence on the behavior of the criminal justice system and the
potential for damaging social trust in urban areas.

We believe Marc Riedel has written a book that will be an
obligatory reference for scholars working in the area of criminal
violence. This book marks an excellent beginning to the series.

Frank P. Williams III
Marilyn D. McShane

DEDICATED TO

Lillie M. Lockhart

AND

Lillian L. Lockhart

TABLE OF CONTENTS

PREFACE

This book originated with a paper delivered at a Western Society of Criminology meeting. One of the panel members was Gilbert Geis. After the panel presentation, I gave a copy of the paper to Gil and asked him to provide me with suggestions as to how the paper might be improved for publication. After reading it, he suggested that it should be turned into a book. Gil has been consistently helpful and patiently edited a very large number of revisions as I tried to work out the implications of the original set of ideas. What merit this volume has is largely a tribute to Gil's marvelous skill as an editor. I thank him for his efforts.

I am grateful also to Julian Roebuck who provided many helpful suggestions after reviewing an early version of this book. In the course of developing the manuscript, Roger Przybylski and I presented a paper at an American Society of Criminology meeting. Julian was a discussant on the panel and offered a variety of helpful suggestions that found their way into the following pages.

James Short also reviewed an early version of the book. His suggestions on micro-level and macro-level theories were extremely useful in revising the manuscript.

Robert Silverman and Terence Thornberry provided detailed evaluations of various parts of the manuscript. Bob kept the BITNET line between Edmonton and Carbondale humming with additional help, support, and jokes, as the manuscript developed. Thanks, guys!

I appreciate the opportunity Frank Williams and Marilyn McShane have given me to publish this volume in their series. They, as well as Paula Ladenburg and Eunice Petrini at Garland Publishing, have provided many helpful suggestions in revising the final manuscript.

Graduate students, and former graduate students, have provided various kinds of useful assistance. Leading this group was Roger

Przybylski, now at the Illinois Criminal Justice Information Authority, who did a thesis that provided many useful insights into the question of stranger violence. Sue Speers carefully summarized stranger murder cases from the nationwide study on homicide. As will be seen at various points in the book, these "cases" usefully served to illustrate theoretical concepts. Finally, my graduate assistants, Tim Rodgers, Janelle Miller, and Stacey E. Grinnell labored over the final draft looking for typographical errors, inconsistent conclusions, and ambiguous sentences.

Early in the preparation of this manuscript, Michael R. Dingerson, Director of the Office of Research Development and Administration at Southern Illinois University, provided me with a number of small grants to carry out the theoretical and empirical research reported here. Mike has since moved on to become Associate Vice Chancellor for Research and Dean of the Graduate School at the University of Mississippi. Without his support, the preliminary research needed for this project would not have been possible.

James Fox, Catherine Martinsek, and Walter Stubbs of Morris Library spent a great deal of time doing computerized searches and interlibrary loans for this book. Walter Stubbs made his way through government documents with ease to find what I needed. I would also like to thank Linda Patrick and her staff in the Operations Support Center at Southern Illinois University for a really fine job of turning the typescript into camera-ready copy.

Finally, I would like to thank Lillie M. Lockhart and her mother, Lillian L. Lockhart, for their support. As promised, this book is dedicated to them.

Villa Capri
Phoenix, Arizona
July, 1991

CHAPTER 1

STRANGERS AND STRANGER VIOLENCE

INTRODUCTION

Most violence involves a prior relationship between the victim and offender. A husband may return home late one night to find his wife in a rage over what she believes is his persistent infidelity. An argument ensues, threats and counter-threats are made, a weapon is drawn, and one of the participants is injured or dies. Or to take another example, two men are drinking and in the course of the evening one makes some disparaging or insulting remarks about the other's girlfriend or wife. The two argue loudly, a fight ensues, one of the participants is injured and subsequently dies of his injuries.

The examples are typical in the realm of criminal violence. Most murders grow out of disputes or disagreements and most occur between people who knew one another before the fatal event. Indeed, between sixty-five and eighty percent of all urban homicides recorded by the police involve victims and offenders known to each other.[1] Many aggravated assaults, rapes and some robberies also involve victims and offenders who had a relationship prior to the violent event.

This is a book about a form of violence which, while occurring somewhat less often, is more frightening. This is a study of crimes in which victim and offender were personally unknown to each other. Because such violence involves strangers, the physical violence does not emerge out of long-suppressed feelings of hatred, jealousy, or resentment. Rather, violent encounters between strangers erupt quickly, almost

1

accidentally, often out of attempts to commit robbery or rape. Here is an example:

> The victim was a 19-year-old white gas station attendant who was working, together with the older station manager, on the graveyard shift. The killer, a 20-year-old black male, drove up to the station requesting a fill-up. The killer and his companion, who later was apprehended but not prosecuted, left their car at the gasoline pumps and went into the station. One of them suddenly pointed a gun at the two gas station attendants. He demanded all the money in the cash register. As the younger man began to open the cash register he accidentally broke off the handle. He put the handle in his back pocket and that action was taken by the killer to mean that the attendant was going for a gun. The killer fired his .22 caliber pistol and the 19-year-old gas station attendant fell over dead. The killer and his companion . . . emptied the cash register and left the station with their haul, which amounted to $80. (Lundsgaarde, 1977: 135-136)

Stranger murders, however, do not always occur in conjunction with another felony. A substantial number develop on the streets or out of conflicts in recreational settings, such as bars. Commonly a fatal outcome develops from what seems to be a very trivial incident. Here is a police report of such an incident:

> At 5:10 P.M. police responded to a call to investigate a possible fight. Upon arrival police found the victim, a 28-year-old white male, lying in the street. Reports indicated that the victim pulled up to an intersection which was blocked by vehicles and pedestrians. The victim honked the horn several times at which time several individuals began beating the victim's car with baseball bats. The victim got out of the car to protest their actions and the same individuals began beating him with baseball bats. The victim died as a result of his injuries.[2]

While stranger violence represents a smaller proportion of criminal violence than that between persons known to each other, its effects are disproportionately greater. Stranger murders and violence represent one of the most frightening forms of criminal victimization. Indeed, Conklin (1975) and McIntyre (1967) have argued that the fear of crime is, at bottom, a fear of strangers. There are, it is suggested, three components to the fear of stranger violence: settings, behavior, and people.

Some settings are more fear-provoking than others. To be a tourist on the streets of Beirut, Lebanon, during the current violent hostilities is to be in a more fear-provoking setting than being a tourist in St. Louis, Missouri. Because much stranger violence occurs in public settings, streets and other public locations are more frightening than a person's home. The fear is independent of what the person may be doing in the setting. The Beirut tourist may be taking photographs of buildings when he or she is killed. The ordinary citizen may be going about his or her routine daily activities when he or she is the victim of a violent and unpredictable attack.

Second, when violent victimization is a possibility, the capability of expressing behavior that reduces the risk also reduces the fear. There is, apparently, less fear associated with violent behavior when the person is behaving in a way that gives him or her the feeling of a measure of control. The popularity of home-security devices, self-defense courses, Mace, various kinds of stun guns and handguns are ways that people attempt to protect themselves against violent victimization. Even robbery offenders, according to Walsh (1986), were fearful of injury and death before the event. However, once the robbery was underway, the anxiety was reduced.

By contrast, knowing that one can be victimized and also knowing that there is little that can be done to prevent it is very fear provoking. What makes stranger violence especially frightening is that the victim feels he or she has little control over events. Paradoxically, as will be seen in the following chapters, the crime treated most seriously by the criminal justice process, stranger homicide, is often the one that is caused by the most trivial of events. Arguments over a parking space, the ownership of a can of beer, whether a person was intentionally jostled in a bar, or almost anything else can erupt with surprising suddenness into violence. However compliant a victim may be in a robbery, his behavior may be misinterpreted by the offender with fatal results. Such encounters generate high anxiety because the victim feels that nothing that he or she does can prevent violence and anything may provoke it.

Finally, stranger violence is frightening because we are often in the presence of persons who may launch an indiscriminate attack. The omnipresence of strangers leads to a "startling paradox":

Life in metropolitan areas . . . involves a startling paradox: we fear strangers more than anything else, and yet we live our lives among strangers. Every time we take a walk, ride a subway or bus, shop in a supermarket or department store, enter an office building lobby or elevator, work in a factory or large office, or attend a ball game or the movies, we are surrounded by strangers. The potential for fear is as immense as it is unavoidable. (Silberman, 1978:11)

The fear of crime from strangers has important consequences for life in a civil society. People stay behind locked doors and travel by taxi or car rather than public transportation or on foot to avoid contact with strangers. When people go out, they travel in groups and avoid returning to their homes at a late hour. They stay away from cultural and educational events if it means traveling to a certain section of the city at night. Such avoidance behavior represents what economists call "opportunity costs." When people stay home they are not enjoying the educational and cultural advantages of their community. By restricting who they will interact with, they decrease the general level of sociability. Such responses not only undermine the trust essential for a civil society, but diminish the quality of life as well (Conklin, 1975; McIntyre, 1967).

It might be supposed that because of its terrifying nature, the phenomena of stranger violence would be well understood. Such is not the case. Stranger violence has been the subject of some empirical inquiries, but what is surprising is the inattentiveness to basic issues. What is the amount and rate of stranger violence? What is meant by the term "stranger"? Are there different kinds of stranger relationships? What is the difference between routine and violent encounters with strangers? These are key questions that have gone unanswered.

The present volume seeks to take some important steps toward understanding stranger violence. The focus in this volume will be on the basic issues of description, definition, and classification. Within that context, the following two chapters examine empirical and methodological questions related to the measurement of stranger violence in order to determine the incidence and rates of these violent events. Those readers who are more interested in theoretical matters should skip to Chapter 4 which is a discussion of the meaning of the term "stranger" and a review of theories of stranger behavior. Beginning with Chapter 5, an alternative formulation of stranger relationships is presented which suggests that stranger violence emerges out of routine encounters in settings that are exploited or manipulated for violent ends. Chapter 6 explores in detail two different forms of stranger violence while Chapter 7 examines the consequences of these two forms for the processing of offenders by criminal justice organizations.

STRANGERS: THEN AND NOW

Strangers pose a major problem for the continuing existence of groups. Because socialization is what makes human animals social persons, the appearance of someone socialized in quite a different way can be tantamount, from the group's point of view, to interacting with someone who is not socialized at all. Such a simple outlook toward strangers is, perhaps, most applicable to preliterate groups where the societies are small, isolated, and homogeneous. Strangers pose a threat because they can intentionally or accidentally profane sacred values by their behavior. Becker and Barnes note that the aversion to strangers practiced by preliterate tribes is not necessarily directed at the stranger as such. Rather, in a culture with a multiplicity of taboos and restrictions, "even the most amiable of strangers might commit sacrilege every time he turned around; only long training by some preliterate friend . . . could save him from the deadly social-religious blunder." (Becker and Barnes, 1961:14) It is easy to understand why preliterate tribes would view the stranger as the source of unpredictable and possibly dangerous behavior.

Lofland (1973) has characterized the stranger as an "exceptional person" meaning that in preliterate and contemporary rural societies, the appearance of a stranger was an unusual occasion. Routine activities were brought to a halt until the stranger appearance was dealt with. In some instances, the stranger was killed. Lofland (1973) suggests that among the Tiwi, such a tradition was firm and certain. People who came from the outside and were not part of Tiwi culture were viewed as dangerous and were massacred or vigorously resisted.

In other cases, the appearance of the stranger aroused feelings of awe in preliterate minds. There is a saying among the Ainu: "Do not treat strangers slightingly for you never know whom you are entertaining" (Wood, 1934: 79). Strangers were viewed with respect and honor because they may be gods in disguise. Westermarck and Briffault suggest that the view of the stranger as a possible god in disguise may explain the rites of sacred prostitution among uncultured peoples and in the ancient world. Men who participated in these rites were explicitly described as strangers (Wood, 1934).

In the history of the United States, differences in the treatment of strangers were a consequence of attitudes and laws toward outsiders (Rothman, 1971). Among American pioneer settlers, hospitality toward strangers was an important norm, perhaps because the hosts could remember their own difficult trek westward. In her study of Kansas pioneer women, Stratton (1981) notes that their hospitable and warm nature was not without caution. She quotes from one of the letters of Kate Aplington:

> I was alone all day, and half frightened lest vicious-minded stragglers might annoy me. I had no gun, but kept a cup of cayenne pepper and a corn-knife within reach. I knew I could make things hot and interesting for a tramp. (Stratton, 1981: 130)

The caution expressed toward a stranger was sometimes well founded. In one of the records of pioneer life, a woman named Theoline Plummer writes:

> One evening at dusk, a tall, ungainly-looking woman, queerly dressed, carrying a heavy satchel, came to our door and asked permission to stay all night. She said she was alone and did not like to stay at the hotel. She looked tired and travel strained. I told her to come in. Soon afterward, she asked permission to go to bed. When the Doctor [Theoline's husband] returned from the country, he thought she must be a queer duck, but probably she was all right. She guardedly kept her satchel near her head so that she could readily place her hand on it. When we got up in the morning, she was gone. A short time afterward, we learned that our strange visitor was the noted bandit, Jesse James, in disguise. (Stratton, 1981:130-131)

In preliterate and rural societies, where everyone is personally known, the appearance of a stranger meant that routine activities were stopped until the stranger could be identified and placed in a social category. All this changed, of course, with the appearance of cities.

A city is a place where the vast majority of people know nothing personally about others with whom they share space. For the average urban dweller, meeting and interacting with strangers is a routine fact of life. A central problem in urban settings is ordering our interaction with strangers because, if for no other reason, there are so many of them. Citing a study by a New York agency, Milgram states:

> In Nassau County, a suburb of New York City, an individual can meet 11,000 others within a 10-minute radius of his office by foot or car. In Newark, a moderate-sized city, he can meet more than 20,000 persons within this radius. But in midtown Manhattan he can meet fully 220,000. (Milgram, 1970: 1461)

In addition, there are biophysical limitations to the number of people who may be known by name or face. While Lofland (1973) "guesses" that the maximum number might be three or four thousand, the point is that the number of strangers and, therefore, stranger encounters in a city far exceeds a person's capacity for personal knowledge.

Third, there are structural limitations to knowing personally a large number of people. In a highly complex and differentiated city, a person's routine behavior becomes restricted, so that the opportunity to interact with others is limited. A housewife, for example, meets fewer strangers than her corporate executive husband. Warehouse clerks interact with fewer strangers than street-corner vendors.

Finally, there are time limitations to knowing people. Cities have traditionally been places of transients; people come, conduct their business, and move on, limiting the number of encounters with the same people (Lofland, 1973).

With the appearance of large numbers of strangers in cities, there is a shift in the focus of interaction from actors to acts. In preliterate societies, it was the strangers themselves who were the subject of scrutiny and suspicion; in modern societies, there is more concern with what strangers will do.

The change from actors to acts does not lessen the amount of fear of strangers, but it does change how the urban dweller acts. The urban dweller uses knowledge about strangers and how he or she should act to minimize or control interaction with them. One way this is done is by transforming urban public space.

Transforming public space refers to the strategies the urban dweller uses to convert public into private or semiprivate space. Such transformations can be either locational or symbolic. Locational transformation refers to the actual changes in the character of a location achieved with the help of others or technology. One of the more interesting devices to transform public spaces is the automobile. The urban dweller, by using the automobile, can move around the city and need only rarely enter public space. He or she is encased in a cocoon of private space in which they can go from their home to their workplace, to the homes of friends and back without physically encountering any strangers.

Symbolic transformations of public space occur when the urbanite uses body management and facial expressions to create around himself a shield of privacy. By minimizing facial expressions and body contact, choosing locations to sit, and "disattending" to others in a public setting, the urban dweller communicates to strangers that he or she does not want to interact with them (Lofland, 1973).

In her ethnographic study of danger in an ethnically mixed housing project, Engle Merry (1981) confirms many of Lofland's concepts. Chinese, blacks, and whites of Dover Square, the name she gives to the housing project, characterize strangers in broad social categories. Where ethnic groups live in uneasy proximity with little communication among them, the categories are primarily ethnically linked. Strangers are likely to be perceived as dangerous, unpredictable, and difficult to control. Thus, among the Chinese, who interact with other ethnic groups the least, blacks and whites "all look alike." Additionally, they are perceived as dangerous and untrustworthy. Whites, according to Engle Merry, are able to identify some members of other ethnic groups who commit crimes in Dover Square. It is, however, the blacks who are most skilled at drawing distinctions among strangers because they interact most frequently with members of other ethnic groups.

Engle Merry (1981) found that with respect to symbolic transformations, effective strategies for dealing with strangers were not limited to efforts to avoid interaction, but included displaying a type of indifference.

One of these is to maintain a determined businesslike manner: an appearance of self-confidence and strength, and a studied indifference to the safety of pockets and purses where money could be concealed send off signals that a person is a poor choice as a victim. The self-presentation should indicate that this person will resist if attacked. Any indication of fear, timidity or clutching of purse or pocket communicate the opposite: fear and something to hide. (Engle Merry, 1981: 175)

Finally, in more urbanized societies with highly developed formal systems of social control, strangers are more frequently subject to these systems than nonstrangers. In her anthropological study of an isolated rural fishing community, "Rock Island,"[3] Yngvesson (1978) found the way a "grievance" developed depended on the nature of the relationship between the parties. She cited the case of Albert Cooper, a long-time native of Rock Island. During Yngvesson's residence, Albert had taken to giving swimming lessons to young girls, but insisted that they swim nude. Despite the fact that the girls complained to their parents and the parents expressed concern, nothing was done. One mother said, "He is that way," while another said, "It is an illness." At the time Yngvesson left, no action was planned against Albert by the islanders.

In contrast, there was a dispute over land rights by fishermen, who had been on the island for generations, and descendants of the lighthouse keepers who were not viewed as members of the community. The descendants laid claim to land on which the lighthouse had formerly stood, along with the surrounding area; the fishermen believed the land belonged to them. Rather than reaching an informal resolution in the community, the case was brought to court.

A PERSPECTIVE ON VIOLENCE

An important first step in understanding stranger violence is to determine the incidence of murders and other forms of stranger violence. A comparison of Supplementary Homicide Reports, provided as part of the Uniform Crime Reports, with similar information on victim/offender relationships available from city police departments, indicated a consistent pattern of underreporting at the national level. While the Uniform Crime Reports indicated that 13.2 percent of reported homicides in 1987 involved strangers, the analysis presented in Chapter 2 indicated that stranger homicides make up at least 25 percent of reported homicides. Rather than ranking last in the type of homicide committed, the latter analysis indicated that stranger homicides were more frequent than homicides involving family members.

An inability to obtain valid estimates of the number of stranger homicides from Uniform Crime Reports is paralleled by a similar lack of accurate information on other forms of stranger violence. A Bureau of Justice Statistics report (1987) indicated that 57 percent of rapes, robberies, and assaults were committed by strangers. Yet, as the analysis in Chapter 3 indicates, this percentage is inflated because of underreporting by victims of nonstranger violence. While there have been guesses and speculation that the nonstranger rate of violence is much higher than reported by victimization survey, no valid or reliable nationwide estimates exist.

In addition to not being able to ascertain the amount of stranger violence, there are more serious problems related to conceptualization. There is a tendency to equate stranger violence with robberies and robbery homicides. A large proportion of robberies do involve strangers: Zimring and Zuehl (1986) report than 87 percent of the 360 robberies in Chicago were by stranger perpetrators. This is not true for robbery homicides. As Zimring and Zuehl indicate, only 53 percent of the 95 robbery killings involved strangers.

There are a large number of stranger killings that do not involve robberies. In a study of eight cities, Zahn and Sagi (1987) found that only 57.3 percent of the stranger homicides were felony associated (mostly robberies). The percentages ranged from 50 percent in Oakland, California to 66.7 percent in Newark, New Jersey.

On the face of it, it is less than adequate science to use robbery murder as an indicator of stranger involvement in violence when it captures only about half of its most serious manifestations, i.e., stranger murders. But even this is not clear. The difficulty is that the percentage of robbery murders is calculated on a base of all homicides, which includes the substantial number of cases in which the relationship is unknown (See Chapter 2). For example, in the Zimring and Zuehl study, when the latter cases are excluded (24%), the percentage of robbery murder cases in which the victim and offender had no prior relationship increases to 70 percent.

It is obvious that the cases with unrecorded relationships are important. Based on the analysis in the following chapter, it is reasonable to suppose that many of these cases involve strangers. What complicates the issue is that the evidence also suggests these missing values refer to cases that do not involve robberies (Zimring and Zuehl, 1986).

The problem of measurement and indicators is reinforced, if not caused, by few theoretical efforts to explain stranger violence. Existing theories can be divided into those that explain stranger relationships, discussed in Chapter 4, and those that explain violence. A criminological perspective that is consistent with the view that robberies are an indicator of stranger violence has been developed by Block (1977). A current statement of the precipitating crime perspective is given by C. R. Block.

Homicide is not one crime, but several kinds of crime, each of which has unique characteristics. A homicide may begin as an assault (fight, brawl or argument) and escalate to murder; or it may begin as a robbery, burglary, or rape, and then escalate to murder. An occasional homicide---such as a contractual killing---has no motive other than the murder itself, but these cases are very infrequent. Most homicides are precipitated by some other crime, and are more similar in their characteristics to that other crime than to other types of homicides. . . . Homicides that begin as assaults differ from homicides that begin as robberies in a number of ways, including place and time of occurrence, victim-offender relationship, and many other characteristics. . . . In fact, homicides that begin as assaults are more similar in their characteristics to aggravated assaults than they are to homicides that begin as robberies. . . . They almost can be considered to be separate types of crime. A homicide that begins as a fight or brawl can be thought of as a type of aggravated assault, one in which the victim was injured so seriously that death resulted. (Block, 1987: 34)

Using the precipitating crime perspective, Block provides an analysis of 12,872 homicides from 1965 through 1981. The difficulty with this perspective is not with the extensive and detailed findings provided by Block. Current descriptive research on homicides is very much needed in the field (Riedel, 1989). The difficulty is that Block seems to generalize beyond what is warranted by the data in discussing victim/offender relationships.

Thus, these two aspects of the homicide situation--- victim/offender relationship and [precipitating] circumstance---are different. To use them as if they were interchangeable---to assume, for example, that all homicides between acquaintances are impulsive[4] and all homicides between strangers are instrumental---would be to misrepresent the truth. Of the two aspects, we have found circumstance to be, by far, the more fundamental---a basic variable to which everything else, including relationship is secondary. (C. R. Block, 1987: 35)

It is clear that precipitating crime circumstances and victim/offender relationships are different variables. What is difficult to understand is how precipitating crime is the more "fundamental" variable. Without empirical research that clearly differentiates stranger and felony violence and establishes causal priority, such a conclusion is premature.

In a newspaper interview in 1985, Zimring rather colorfully indicated that victim/offender relationships need to be examined much more carefully. "What the hell is stranger-to-stranger violence? We need to know who these strangers are and why the rate is going up." (Meredith, 1989: D1)

One year later, Zimring and Zuehl suggest that stranger relationships are less important. "The 'stranger' label, while not meaningless, conveys only a single distinction where many distinctions and differences are necessary to understanding patterns of homicide." (Zimring and Zuehl, 1986: 29)

The problem, it seems, is not with the answers, but with the questions. It is impossible to understand stranger violence or assess the utility of the idea until there is a theoretical formulation that addresses the phenomena. Theory is a construction of reality and its value is evaluated by its consequences and comparisons with other theories. To question the value of the victim/offender relationship because it does not fit conveniently into a perspective that reflects legal categories of assaults and robberies suggests a need for an alternative theory.

The problem was addressed by Sellin in his discussion of the nature of a scientific criminology. Sellin objected to the unqualified acceptance of legal definitions as the basic element of criminological inquiry because it violates a fundamental criterion of science.

> The scientist must have freedom to define his own terms, based on the intrinsic character of his material and designating properties in that material which are assigned to be universal. . . . It should be emphasized at this point that the above comments do not imply that the criminal law or the data about crimes and criminals assembled in the process of its enforcement are not useful in scientific research. They are indeed a rich source for the scientist, but the application of scientific criteria to the selection and classification of these data independently of their legal form is essential to render them valuable to science. . . . The data of the criminal law and the data about crimes and criminals now subservient to legal categories must be "processed" by the scientist before he can use them. (Sellin, 1938: 23-25)

Such "processing" implies that criminologists have developed theories that provide hypotheses different from those that could be generated from a legal perspective. The task, Sellin implies, is to develop theoretical approaches and categories that can make use of data generated by criminal law without being dominated by latter's conceptual categories. In other words, what must be avoided, on the one hand, are theories of deviance that cannot use criminal justice data and, on the other hand, theories that are so similar to criminal justice concepts that no different questions emerge. Perhaps because of the current concern for the policy relevance of criminological research, there is more danger that criminological theory will become the conceptual handmaiden of a legal perspective than that it will develop theories independent of data generated by the criminal justice process.

Clearly, what is called for is a conceptualization of stranger violence that focuses on the basic problems of definition and classification. While the outcome of this effort will be exploratory and preliminary rather than definitive, it should serve the heuristic purpose of forming a basis for discussion, research, and further theorizing on the phenomena.

Conceptualizing Stranger Violence

There are several considerations that have guided the construction of a theoretical perspective on stranger violence. An initial problem centered on the definition of a stranger relationship. Nearly all criminological writings have made use of negative definitions, i.e., stranger offenders are those with no prior relationship to the victims. While such a definition suffices for empirical research, it is difficult, if not impossible, to theorize about an entity that is defined exclusively in terms of some other entity or entities. It is like defining the term "enemy" as "not a friend" and comparing it exclusively to the category of "friend." On the other hand, sociological theorists who have considered the phenomena of strangers do provide a positive definition of the category. The difficulty is that much of what they have to say has few direct implications for contemporary urban stranger violence.

The latter difficulties are resolved to some extent by the view that stranger violence emerges from routine stranger relationships. Thus, it is necessary to not only explain the "world of strangers" (Lofland, 1973), but to show how routine stranger relationships are manipulated for violent ends.

Block has suggested that "most killing[s] are the outcome of either an aggravated assault or a robbery which somehow progressed beyond the degree of harm intended by the offender" (Block, 1977: 10). Because of research showing similarities between aggravated assaults and homicides (Curtis, 1974; Pittman and Handy, 1964; Pokorny, 1965), it followed that the situations or settings in which the crimes occurred were of little etiological significance. The focus, instead, should be on the similarities and differences between homicides that begin as aggravated assaults and those that begin as robberies.

The latter conclusion does not necessarily follow from the view that homicide results from events that "somehow progressed beyond the degree of harm intended by the offender." It is equally logical to consider what those events were in the setting that led to the fatal outcome. Some are, of course, related to chance. How swiftly medical help is provided to a gunshot victim, the proximity of a hospital to a violent scene, and even the firearms proficiency of the offender helps to determine whether the victim is injured or dies.

But there are many other features of a setting that aid in determining a fatal or non-fatal outcome. If there were not, it would be meaningless for criminologists and crime prevention groups to advise the citizen victim to be calm and offer no resistance in robberies. If the event is determined by chance outcomes largely external to the setting, why bother? In her study of felony homicides, Lorenz Dietz put the matter well:

> In any given homicide, the reality of perception and the motives attributed to the various participants are contingent upon the particular situation. Throughout the homicide, there are negotiations within the killer group itself, between the killers and between the killers and their victims. Life and death hangs in the balance during these interactions. (Lorenz Dietz, 1983:162)

Because violent encounters between strangers develop out of routine settings and because what happens in these encounters has a great deal to do with whether the outcome is fatal, the present exposition focuses on the interaction between strangers both before and during these events.

Whether the violent event was committed by strangers is an important dimension in explaining the responses of criminal justice agencies. In comparison with violence among nonstrangers, violence among strangers is treated as a more serious offense by law enforcement, prosecutors, and courts. This means that it is necessary to consider what a theory of stranger violence implies in terms of a criminal justice response. This is discussed in detail in the last chapter.

Finally, the more severe treatment meted out to stranger offenders by agents of the criminal justice process is paralleled by concern and fear expressed by the public about this phenomena. Given the latter, it is one of the anomalies of stranger violence that it has generated little research or theory among criminologists who focus on explaining patterns of violence surrounding the event itself. Hopefully, the present inquiry will help provide an understanding of the gap between public fears and legal responses.

NOTES

1. In studying homicide, writers are frequently unclear about the use of terms. As Wilbanks (1982) has noted, some writers use the terms interchangeably as if the definition were the same. In general, homicide is the more inclusive term covering both criminal and noncriminal homicide. Murder is a subset of criminal homicide that involves both intent and premeditation. For a description of the terms and a discussion of the problems, see Wolfgang (1958). In the present volume, the term "murder" seems to most accurately encompass the variety of criminal homicide that I am interested in describing. Where other research is cited, I will use the term used by the research in reporting the results.

2. Unless otherwise noted, the homicide cases described in this book came from the project, "Nature and Patterns of American Homicide" (LEAA-USDJ 79-NI-AX 0092). The cases were taken from one part of the project, the study of eight American cities. For a report on the nine cities where Margaret Zahn collected data for the project, see Zahn and Sagi (1987). I am grateful to Sue Speers who provided summaries of the cases from information available on the data collection forms.

3. The location is identified only as a "fishing community of 314 persons, located off the Atlantic coast of an industrialized Western nation." (Yngvesson, 1978: 60)

4. Impulsive homicides are those that are not planned in advance while instrumental homicides are planned ahead. (C. R. Block, 1987)

REFERENCES

Becker, H., & Barnes, H. E. (1961). Social Thought from Lore to Science. (Vol. 1). New York: Dover.

Block, R. (1977). Violent crime: Environment, interaction and death. Lexington: Lexington Books.

Block, C. R. (1987). Homicide in Chicago: Aggregate and time series perspectives on victim, offender, and circumstances (1965-1981). Chicago: Loyola University of Chicago.

Bureau of Justice Statistics (1987). Violent crime by strangers and nonstrangers. Washington: U.S. Government Printing Office.

Conklin, J. E. (1975). The Impact of Crime. New York: Macmillan.

Curtis, L. A. (1974). Criminal violence: National patterns and behavior. Lexington: Lexington Books.

Engle Merry, S. (1981). Urban danger: Life in a neighborhood of strangers. Philadelphia: Temple University Press.

Lofland, L. H. (1973). A world of strangers: Order and action in urban public space. New York: Basic Books.

Lorenz Dietz, M. (1983). Killing for profit. Chicago: Nelson-Hall.

Lundsgaarde, H. F. (1977). Murder in space city: A cultural analysis of Houston homicide patterns. New York: Oxford University Press.

McIntyre, J. (1967). Public attitudes toward crime and law enforcement. Annals of the American Academy of Political and Social Science, 374, 34-46.

Meredith, N. (1985). Homicide: Scientists stalk cure for epidemic of violence. The Register, March 5, D1, D5.

Milgram, S. (1970). The experience of living in cities. Science, 167, 1461-1468.

Pittman, D., & Handy, W. (1964). Patterns in criminal aggravated assault. Journal of Criminal Law, Criminology, and Police Science, 55, 462-470.

Pokorny, A. D. (1965). A comparison of homicide in two cities. Journal of Criminal Law, Criminology, and Police Science, 56, 479-487.

Riedel, M. (1989). Book Review of Homicide in Chicago. Criminal Justice Review, 13, in press.

Rothman, D. J. (1971). The discovery of the asylum. Boston: Little, Brown and Co.

Sellin, T. (1938). Culture conflict and crime. New York: Social

Science Research Council.

Silberman, C. E. (1978). Criminal Violence, Criminal Justice. New York: Random House.

Stratton, J. L. (1981). Pioneer women: Voices from the K a n s a s frontier. New York: Simon and Schuster.

Walsh, D. (1986). Heavy business: commercial burglary and robbery. London: Routledge & Kegan Paul.

Wilbanks, W. (1982). Murdered women and women who murder: A critique of the literature. In N. H. Rafter and E. A. Stanko (Eds.), Judge, lawyer, victim, thief: Women, gender roles, and criminal justice (pp. 151-180). Boston: Northeastern University Press.

Wolfgang, M. E. (1958). Patterns in criminal homicide. Philadelphia: University of Pennsylvania Press.

Wood, M. M. (1934). The stranger: A study of social relationships. New York: Columbia University Press.

Yngvesson, B. B. (1978). The Atlantic fisherman. In L. Nader and H. F. Todd, Jr. (Eds.), The disputing process--Law in ten societies (pp. 59-85). New York: Columbia University Press.

Zahn, M. A., & Sagi, P. C. (1987). Stranger homicides in nine American cities. Journal of Criminal Law and Criminology, 78, 377-397.

Zimring, F. E., & Zuehl, J. (1986). Victim injury and death in urban robbery: A Chicago study. Journal of Legal Studies, 15, 1-40.

CHAPTER 2

STRANGER HOMICIDES

A reasonable starting point for understanding homicide and violence involving strangers is to determine how widespread such events are. Among all acts of criminal violence for a given city, what proportion are stranger related? How do such events compare with violence and homicides involving family members and friends and acquaintances? Is stranger violence increasing? This and the following chapter on non-fatal forms of stranger violence aims to answer the preceding questions.

Nationwide estimates must rely on Uniform Crime Reports (UCR) and the Supplementary Homicide Reports (SHR) for data on murder or homicide involving strangers, published annually by the Federal Bureau of Investigation. Before 1976, the SHR reported information on victim/offender relationships as part of other circumstances of the homicide. Trying to determine what part of that reported data related to various types of victim/offender relationships was, however, very difficult and, in the end, not very reliable.

Beginning in 1976, the problem was partly remedied when the SHR was revised by the Uniform Crime Reporting Division and information was collected on victim/offender relationships as a separate variable. However, as will be seen subsequently, when distributions of victim/offender relationships for police department homicides are compared with similar SHR distributions, stranger homicides are systematically underreported. In lieu of SHR data, estimates of the frequency of stranger homicides can be derived from a number of research studies based on police department records. The results suggest that stranger homicides may be increasing and that they are a higher proportion of homicides than indicated by the SHR.

Reporting Homicides and Stranger Homicides

There is general agreement that homicides, including murders, are highly reported and that official data probably are the best source of numerical information. There is a great value placed on human life in our society and the intentional killing of another generally arouses the attention of persons who will report the event to the authorities (Sellin, 1962). Even when homicides are committed in private, they have an intense public aspect. The prolonged unexplained absence of a person attracts the attention of friends, co-workers, neighbors and relatives who are apt to report the "disappearance" to the police. Regardless of the cause of death, the discovery of a dead body invariably mobilizes the substantial resources of the police, coroner, or medical examiner.

Unlike other crimes, homicides are reported by two agencies at both the local and the national levels, thereby making underreporting less likely. The coroner or medical examiner completes a death certificate that is filed with a state Bureau of Vital Statistics. The data on homicides, as well as other causes of death, are then microfilmed and sent to the National Center for Health Statistics (NCHS), Division of Vital Statistics, where they are tabulated and published (Cantor and Cohen, 1980). While the NCHS data have more complete coverage than the Uniform Crime Reporting program, the data are limited to information on homicide victims.[1]

Local law enforcement organizations are also responsible for investigating and reporting homicides. Almost all law enforcement agencies voluntarily cooperate with the Uniform Crime Reporting program administered by the Federal Bureau of Investigation.[2] There are four different measures of the incidence of homicide used by the UCR program, but only the SHR will be considered here.[3]

The UCR program requests that a SHR be completed on each homicide. This form, filed monthly with the UCR, contains information on the age, race, and sex of the victim and offender, type of weapon, victim/offender relationship, and felony or nonfelony involvement. Where multiple victims and offenders are involved in the homicide event, information is collected on each victim and offender. This form is the only national source of data on victim/offender relationships for homicide (Riedel, 1990; Uniform Crime Reporting Handbook, 1981).

In evaluating official statistics derived from local or national agencies, it is useful to draw a distinction between missing cases and missing values. Missing cases refers to the extent to which the records are incomplete with respect to the number of cases. Missing values refers to the extent to which there is incomplete information with respect to a category, item or variable in the records. Thus, when a homicide is not reported, that is a missing case. When the homicide is reported, but there is missing information about the type of victim/offender relationship, that is a missing value.

One way to assess the number and percentage of missing cases and missing values is to compare the SHR distribution of victim/offender relationships to similar distributions derived from urban police departments. The next section examines the agreement between SHR and police department data.

On the Agreement Between Police and SHR Data

Table 2-1 shows a distribution of victim/offender relationships derived from the SHR for murder and nonnegligent manslaughter in the United States from 1976 through 1989.

The table indicates that, nationally, murders and nonnegligent manslaughters involving strangers decreased from 18.4 percent in 1976 to 13.3 percent in 1980, but then increased to 17.6 percent in 1984. By 1989, homicides of strangers had declined to 13.1 percent.

Homicides involving family members decreased from 1976 (27.2%) to 1981 (16.9%), increased to 18.7 percent in 1982 and 1983, then decreased to 14.6 percent by 1989. Homicides of friends and acquaintances decreased from 54.4 percent in 1976 to 34.8 percent in 1980, increased to 41.5 percent by 1986, then decreased to 39.2 percent in 1989. Nationwide, victim/offender relationships in which the relationship is unknown increased from 27.0 percent in 1977 to 35.8 percent in 1980, declined to 25.8 percent in 1984, then increased to over 33 percent by 1989.

In comparing categories of victim/offender relationships throughout the nation, there is a question whether the basis of comparison is valid for the three categories.[4] Unlike homicides involving family members and friends and acquaintances, stranger relationships themselves are not

Table 2-1
Victim/Offender Relationships for Murder and
Nonnegligent Manslaughter
1976-1989*

Victim/Offender Relationships**

Year	Family	Friends and Acquaintances	Strangers	Unknown
1976	27.2	54.4	18.4	---
1977	19.4	40.4	13.4	27.0
1978	18.6	37.6	13.5	30.1
1979	16.8	35.2	12.5	35.3
1980	16.1	34.8	13.3	35.8
1981	16.9	37.9	15.5	29.6
1982	18.7	38.3	15.0	28.2
1983	18.7	38.3	15.0	28.2
1984	17.5	39.0	17.6	25.8
1985	17.3	41.3	14.5	26.9
1986	15.7	41.5	13.0	29.8
1987	16.5	40.4	13.2	29.6
1988	15.3	39.6	12.4	32.8
1989	14.6	39.2	13.1	33.1

*Taken from annual editions of <u>Crime in the United States</u>.
**Due to rounding, percentages may not add up to 100.0%

distributed evenly throughout the population. It is commonplace to interact with family and friends in Tipton, Kansas, a small rural town, and unusual to deal with strangers. By contrast, stranger relationships for a resident of Philadelphia are more numerous than nonstranger ones. Given the discrepancy in the opportunities for interaction with strangers, national data on stranger homicides are not truly comparable to similar data for family, friends, and acquaintances.

Even if comparisons are limited to urban areas, there are serious deficiencies in the SHR reports of stranger homicide. This is illustrated in a study of stranger homicides in Memphis. Starting in 1977, the Memphis Police Department developed the Homicide Investigation Data Index (HEIDI), a computerized data base of all homicides in that city from 1974 through 1978. The purpose was to create a means to better manage homicide investigations and to improve suspect identification methods[5] (HEIDI Manual, ND). Because much of the computer work involved a fellow faculty member at the Center for the Study of Crime, Delinquency and Corrections, I became aware of the project as a source of data for a study of stranger homicide.

I made comparisons to determine agreement between several variables available from SHR tapes for Memphis and the HEIDI data (Riedel, 1981). The agreement between the two data sources was acceptable for most of the variables. There were, however, some sharp discrepancies in comparisons of victim/offender relationship distributions.

To measure agreement, the frequency reported by the SHR was divided by the frequency recorded by the city police. Where the frequencies of the two data sources agree completely, the agreement ratio is 1.00. Where the SHR reports a higher frequency than the city police, the ratio is greater than one; where the SHR underreports the frequency, relative to what is recorded by the city police, the agreement ratio is less than one. The agreement ratios comparing Memphis police data to similar data on the SHR are given in Table 2-2.

The table shows that for every type of victim/offender relationship, the city police recorded more homicides than reported by the SHR. The three types of relationships, however, differ substantially among themselves. Among family homicides, Table 2-2 shows that the police recorded 65 homicides while the SHR reported 61 cases. The agreement ratio of .94 indicates that the SHR reported almost 94 percent of the homicides recorded by the police. For friends and acquaintance homicides, there is somewhat greater underreporting than for family homicides; for homicides in the former category, the agreement ratio is

.86. However, the underreporting is greatest for stranger homicides with an agreement ratio of .46. In other words, while the SHR reported almost 94 percent of the family homicides, it tabulated only 46 percent of the stranger homicides. In this initial study, the number of missing cases was not examined. In organizing the data set for a study of stranger homicides, only those cases were included for which there was complete information on victim/offender relationships (Riedel, 1981).

Table 2-2

Victim/Offender Relationships
As Reported by Memphis Police and SHR
(1976-1978)

Victim/Offender Relationships	Memphis		SHR		Agreement Ratio
	freq.	%	freq.	%	
Family	65	19.4	61	23.1	.94
Friends and Acquaintances	193	57.4	167	63.3	.86
Strangers	78	23.2	36	13.6	.46
Total	336	100.0	264	100.0	

The underreporting of stranger homicides by the SHR appears to be the result of two factors: (1) the time required to complete a homicide investigation and (2) the procedures used to update SHR reports. Homicide investigators obtain information on victim/offender relationships by interviewing friends, family members, or others who witnessed the offense or who knew the offender. In family homicides the offender is invariably easily identified or located and can supply information about the relationship to the victim. By contrast, although stranger homicides are very often observed (Zahn and Sagi, 1987), a cooperative network apparently is not available. This means that the police must do more extensive investigation or wait for information from other sources. For example, an undercover narcotics agent may, while working on an unrelated case, hear an offender brag about how he murdered some individual in a city some time previously. This information is shared with homicide detectives and provides them with a suspect for the stranger homicide. In short, the identification of a victim/offender relationship is more time consuming for stranger relationships than for homicides involving family, friends, or acquaintances.

Supplementary Homicide Reports are transmitted to the UCR program each month. If information is not available on victim/offender relationships when the SHR form is completed, that category is recorded as unknown and reported as such by the UCR program. The police may continue their investigation of the stranger homicide after the SHR is filed. Eventually, they may arrest an offender and update their file, but without providing the information to the UCR program. Thus, when comparisons are made between city and SHR data, there almost inevitably will be many fewer stranger homicides reported in the UCR than recorded by the police.

These circumstances suggest that a testable dimension is the time between the occurrence of the event and the identification of a suspect. There should be a longer period of time involved in stranger homicides than homicides involving family or friends and acquaintances. Using the HEIDI data, this is what Table 2-3 illustrates.

Table 2-3 supports the hypothesis that stranger homicides require more time to identify an offender than homicides involving nonstrangers. In all family-related homicides, the suspect had been identified within 24 hours. For the same period the identification of the offender has been learned in 84.1 percent of the friend and acquaintance, and 69.2 percent of the stranger homicides. To put the matter another way, 6.6 percent of the friend and acquaintance, 11.5 percent of the stranger, and none of the family homicides required more than one week to clear.

Table 2-3

Amount of Time Between Event and Identification
of Offender by Victim/Offender Relationship

Time	Family		Friends and Acquaintances		Strangers	
	f	%	f	%	f	%
Less than 24 hours	64	100	153	84.1	36	69.2
24 hours to one week	0	0	17	9.3	10	19.2
Over one week	0	0	12	6.6	6	11.5
Total	64	100	182	100.0	52	100.0

More current research by Zimring and Zeuhl provides additional support. In their study of robbery and robbery murders, Zimring and Zuehl (1986) found that stranger involvement reduces the clearance percentage. Sixty-eight percent of the cleared police-classified robbery murders involved prior relationships, but only 52 percent of stranger robbery murders were cleared by arrest.

The results in Table 2-3 are consistent with the view that stranger homicides in Memphis require a longer time to investigate and that information on the relationship is not systematically reported by the SHR. But such an analysis pertains, after all, to only one city. To establish a pattern of underreporting, similar results must be found in many sites. Fortunately, the data are available for comparisons in eight widely separated American cities.

Victim/Offender Relationships in Other Cities

While doing a study of national homicide patterns, Margaret Zahn and I collected detailed data on homicides for 1978 in eight American cities selected for geographic representativeness and crime trends (Riedel and Zahn, 1985). This data is used here to replicate the earlier finding in Memphis. Table 2-4 compares the city and SHR data on victim/offender relationships for seven cities. Chicago was excluded for two reasons. First, Chicago was the only city where we selected a sample rather than taking the total population of homicides; including Chicago in Table 2-4 would mean comparing sample frequencies to those available from a population. Second, data on all homicides in Chicago were available from another investigator; these comparisons will be discussed subsequently. The pseudonym "Ashton" was given to a western non-California city because of confidentiality requirements imposed by the chief of police of that city.

Table 2-4 shows that among the three types of victim/offender relationships, the city police consistently record more stranger homicides than the SHR. For six of the seven cities, excluding Dallas, the agreement ratios were smaller for stranger homicides than for either of the other two types of victim/offender relationships. In addition, the agreement ratios ranged from .07 in Oakland to .97 in Dallas---almost the entire range of agreement. In other words, while the Oakland SHRs only reported about seven percent of the stranger homicides, Dallas reported about 97 percent of them.

The highest agreement between the two data sets for four cities was for homicides involving family members (St. Louis, Oakland, Dallas, and Ashton). The ratios ranged from 1.00 in Ashton to .74 in St. Louis. For unknown reasons, the Memphis SHR reported 1 1/2 times more family homicides than were recorded by city police.

Table 2-4 suggests that agreement ratios for homicides involving friends and acquaintances were highest in Philadelphia, Newark, and Memphis, with St. Louis having the same agreement ratio as family homicides. For Philadelphia, the SHR reported slightly more (1.06) friend and acquaintance homicides than were recorded by the police. The SHR reported as few as 35.3 percent of the friend and acquaintance homicides in Oakland, while it reported all of them in Newark. The SHR uniformly reported more unknown relationships than were recorded by the police. The range was from 1.58 in Philadelphia to 3.04 in Oakland.

Table 2-4

Victim/Offender Relationships as Reported by Seven
City Police Departments and SHR (1978)

Victim/ Offender Relationships	Philadelphia					Newark					St. Louis				
	PD		SHR		Agreement Ratio	PD		SHR		Agreement Ratio	PD		SHR		Agreement Ratio
	f	%	%	f		f	%	%	f		f	%	%	f	
Within Family	46	12.4	11.3	40	0.87	13	11.8	9.2	10	0.77	27	13.0	9.5	20	0.74
Friends and Acquaintances	138	38.4	41.6	147	1.06	32	32.4	29.4	32	1.00	92	44.4	32.4	68	0.74
Strangers	106	29.3	14.7	52	0.49	28	27.4	19.3	21	0.75	37	17.9	8.1	17	0.46
Unknown	72	19.9	32.3	114	1.58	29	28.4	42.2	46	1.59	51	24.6	50.0	105	2.06
Total	362	100.0	100.0	353	0.97	102	100.0	100.0	109	1.07	207	100.0	100.0	210	1.01

Table 2-4 cont'd

Victim/Offender Relationships as Reported by Seven
City Police Departments and SHR (1978)

Victim/ Offender Relationships	Memphis					Dallas					Oakland				
	PD		SHR			PD		SHR			PD		SHR		
	f	%	f	%	Agreement Ratio	f	%	f	%	Agreement Ratio	f	%	f	%	Agreement Ratio
Within Family	16	12.9	23	20.2	1.44	44	18.5	39	16.8	0.89	11	10.2	10	10.4	0.91
Friends and Acquaintances	68	59.5	64	56.1	0.94	95	41.2	78	33.6	0.82	51	53.1	18	18.8	0.35
Strangers	23	19.8	12	10.5	0.52	63	27.0	61	26.3	0.97	14	14.3	1	1.0	0.07
Unknown	9	7.8	15	13.2	1.67	31	13.3	54	23.3	1.74	22	22.4	67	69.8	3.04
Total	116	100.0	114	100.0	0.98	233	100.0	232	100.0	1.00	98	100.0	96	100.0	0.98

Table 2-4 cont'd

Victim/Offender Relationships as Reported by Seven
City Police Departments and SHR (1978)

Ashton

Victim/ Offender Relationships	PD		SHR		Agree- ment Ratio
	f	%	f	%	
Within Family	19	20.0	19	21.6	1.00
Friends and Acquaintances	38	43.3	32	36.4	0.84
Strangers	21	23.3	12	13.6	0.57
Unknown	12	13.3	25	28.4	2.08
Total	90	100.0	88	100.0	0.98

For the seven cities, the pattern of missing values is similar to what was found in the Memphis study: stranger homicides appear to be underreported by the SHR. The SHR does, however, seem to be reasonably complete with respect to the number of cases. The agreement ratios range from .97 in Philadelphia to 1.07 in Newark. The SHR for St. Louis and Newark tend to report slightly more homicides than are recorded by their police department; for the other five cities, there is a slight tendency for the SHR to underreport the number of homicides.

While stranger homicides were underreported in seven cities for one year, it was also found they were underreported for six years in one city. Using data made available by the Statistical Analysis Center of the Illinois Criminal Justice Information Authority,[6] comparisons were made between Chicago police department records and the SHR for the years 1976-1981. The results are given in Table 2-5.

Table 2-5 indicates a pattern of missing values similar to that found in the preceding data sets. For the six-year period in Chicago, stranger homicides are consistently underreported by the largest amount of the three relationship categories. The SHR may report as few as 60 percent

Table 2-5

Victim/Offender Relationships as Reported by Chicago
Police Department and SHR (1976-1981)*

Victim/ Offender Relationships	1976					1977					1978				
	PD		SHR		Agree-ment Ratio	PD		SHR		Agree-ment Ratio	PD		SHR		Agree-ment Ratio
	f	%	f	%		f	%	f	%		f	%	f	%	
Within Family	100	12.2	103	12.7	1.03	116	14.1	114	13.9	0.98	116	14.7	125	15.9	1.00
Friends and Acquaintances	430	52.6	409	50.5	0.95	379	45.9	372	45.4	0.98	335	42.4	322	41.0	0.96
Strangers	145	17.7	111	13.7	0.76	127	15.4	105	12.8	0.83	174	22.0	166	21.2	0.95
Unknown	143	17.5	187	23.1	1.31	203	24.6	229	27.9	1.13	165	20.9	172	21.9	1.04
Total	818	100.0	810	100.0	0.99	825	100.0	820	100.0	0.99	790	100.0	785	100.0	0.99

Table 2-5 cont'd

Victim/Offender Relationships as Reported by Chicago
Police Department and SHR (1976-1981)*

Victim/ Offender Relationships	1979					1980					1981				
	PD		SHR			PD		SHR			PD		SHR		
	f	%	f	%	Agreement Ratio	f	%	f	%	Agreement Ratio	f	%	f	%	Agreement Ratio
Within Family	97	11.4	91	10.6	0.94	93	10.9	92	10.8	0.99	90	10.3	97	11.1	1.08
Friends and Acquaintances	361	42.3	378	44.2	1.05	359	42.1	373	43.6	1.04	321	36.9	378	43.1	1.18
Strangers	214	25.1	167	19.5	0.78	225	26.4	135	15.8	0.60	258	29.6	164	18.7	0.64
Unknown	182	21.3	220	25.7	1.21	176	20.6	255	29.8	1.45	202	23.2	238	27.1	1.18
Total	854	100.0	856	100.0	1.00	853	100.0	855	100.0	1.00	871	100.0	877	100.0	1.01

* Source of Chicago Data: Unpublished analysis, Illinois Criminal Justice Information Authority, of data collected by Carolyn Rebecca Block, Richard L. Block, and Franklin E. Zimring with the help of the Chicago Police Department.

(1980) or as many as 95 percent (1978) of the stranger homicides. In comparison to the results of preceding data sets, the underreporting in Chicago seems to be a less serious problem in that the agreement ratios generally tend to be higher there than was found in other cities. For family homicides, the agreement ratios between police frequencies and SHR frequencies are high, ranging from .94 in 1979 to 1.08 in 1978 and 1981. Unlike results from preceding data sets, the agreement ratios for homicides involving friends and acquaintances tend to be higher: they range from .95 in 1976 to 1.18 in 1981. In addition, there is a slight tendency for the SHR to report more friend and acquaintance homicides than are recorded by the police from 1979-1981. The greatest amount of overreporting in the Chicago data occurs for the unknown category. The agreement ratios range from 1.45 in 1980 to 1.04 in 1978. The pattern of overreporting for the unknown category on the SHR is also consistent with the results of data sets considered earlier.

The results of the seven city data show little disagreement with respect to the number of homicide cases recorded by the police departments and reported by the SHR. A similar conclusion applies to the Chicago data: the agreement ratios for totals range from .990 to 1.007 which suggests very little disagreement between the two data sources.

Correcting for Missing Information

A useful approach to the problem of missing cases and missing values on the SHR has been suggested by Williams and Flewelling (1987). To develop alternative rate calculation procedures to take account of missing values, Williams and Flewelling used a sample of 83,007 incidents of murder and nonnegligent manslaughter in the United States from 1980 through 1984. Only those incidents were considered that involved one offender and one victim. The geographic areas were 168 cities of more than 100,000 population, their respective metropolitan areas (N = 125), the 50 states, and nine geographic regions.

The first rate calculation procedure developed took account of non-reporting of cases on the SHR. It is a ratio of the number of victims reported on Return A to the number of victims reported in the SHR. The adjusted counts are derived by multiplying the unadjusted totals in the SHR by the weighting factor.

The second and third rate calculation procedures focused on victim/offender relationships, although Williams and Flewelling note that other offender characteristics could also be used. The second procedure extrapolates from the known composition of a category of victim/offender relationship to the unknown one. Thus, if 40 percent of the known events involve stranger homicide, then 40 percent of the unknown cases are added to the calculation of the adjusted rate of stranger homicides. The difficulty with this approach is that it assumes the distribution of known characteristics is the same as the distribution of unknown and stranger homicide rates.

To take account of this difficulty, Williams and Flewelling developed a third procedure in which an additional variable, if it could be shown to be related to victim/offender relationships, was added to the calculations. The circumstances of the offense were used for this purpose. The variable consisted of whether the homicide was felony related. The effect of this procedure was to adjust family and acquaintance homicides downward and stranger homicides upward, as theoretically expected.

After constructing unadjusted, adjusted, and circumstance adjusted rates, the authors did bivariate correlations between them for the cities, metropolitan areas, and states. The correlations for the three methods were high, ranging from a low of r = .936 to a high of r = .996.

Regression analysis, using percent poor and percent black, sought to determine if parameter estimates were altered by the estimation procedures. While the correlations changed to some extent, the greatest changes occurred in expected directions for the origin (a) and the regression coefficient (b). They offered the following summary.

To the extent that an investigator's analytical purpose is to determine the absolute amount of change in rates of family, acquaintance, or stranger homicide associated with changes in theoretically relevant variables, these findings suggest that the use of an adjustment procedure is necessary. Moreover, descriptive statistics about the absolute and relative amounts of specific types of homicide are affected in important ways by the adjustment procedures used (e.g., the absolute and relative amount of stranger homicide becomes higher than family homicides). The circumstance adjustment procedure appears most appropriate because it uses an extensive range of data in the SHR to guide the adjustment process, and analyses using the resulting rates reveal predictable empirical patterns. Nonetheless, if an investigator's purpose is merely to determine patterns of association (i.e., direction, significance, or magnitude of an association), then the choice among the rate calculation procedures is not so consequential. (Williams and Flewelling, 1987: 20-21)

Problems of Classification

Besides problems with missing values, there may be a problem for both police departments and the Uniform Crime Reporting Division in classifying stranger homicides. In one of the few studies of its kind, Loftin, Kindley, Norris, and Wiersema (1987) developed an attribute classification of victim/offender relationships. The classification is based on a series of binary decisions about observable and specific criteria of such relationships. The assumption is that, once the decisions are made, a computer can be used to create either simple or complex multidimensional classifications.

To study the reliability of the attribute classification form, Loftin, et al. (1987) compared the coding of victim/offender relationships from police files to codes given by the SHR. Using a traditional format for 194 cases in Baltimore, the authors found that forty of the homicides were classified as stranger homicides by either the SHR or Loftin's coders. However, only 16 (40%) were classified as stranger homicides by both sets of coders. Using the attribute classification form on a random sample of twenty homicides, Loftin, et al. (1987) found that the two coders agreed on 85 percent of the items. Only three of the 20 cases were classified as stranger homicides but the coders completely agreed on their classification.

Conclusions

The research suggests that stranger homicides are pervasively underreported. In an analysis of three independent data sets covering eight different cities, the agreement between police department records and the SHR frequencies is lower for stranger homicides than for the other two victim/offender categories; stranger homicides are, in other words, consistently underreported by the SHR. By contrast, the unknown category of victim/offender relationships is consistently overreported.

It seems likely, on the basis of the same data sets, that missing cases are not a major problem. For seven cities in one year and Chicago for six years, the agreement between the totals for police department and SHR distributions of victim/ offender relationships is high.

A rate calculation procedure such as that proposed by Williams and Flewelling is needed to cope with the problem of missing values in victim/offender relationships. The construction of circumstance adjusted rates is more important for determining the absolute amount of change in offender variables than for descriptive studies or studies attempting to determine the magnitude or direction of association. Unfortunately, no research exploring the utility of these procedures has been conducted.

While the previous research indicates that the SHR is not a very accurate measure of stranger homicide, limited evidence suggests that types of victim/offender relationships have not been reliably classified. Loftin, et al. (1987) research on attribute classification showed that 40 of 194 Baltimore homicides were classified as stranger homicides by two independent groups of coders, but only 16 cases, or 40 percent, were classified as stranger homicides by both.

Based on the victim/offender relationship variable, the SHR may be a relatively accurate measure of the number of homicides, but it is neither an accurate nor reliable measure of the number or proportion of stranger homicides. Given the number of city distributions examined, it is reasonable to suggest that the underreporting of stranger homicides by the SHR is a national pattern. If the SHR cannot be used to ascertain the incidence and direction of stranger homicide, it is necessary to consider how city police homicide records can be employed for that purpose.

AMOUNTS AND CHANGES IN
STRANGER HOMICIDES

If it is assumed that victim/offender relationships found in police records are more complete than SHR records, it is necessary to consider the extent to which independent researchers agree in reporting victim/offender relationships from the same city at the same time. A partial answer can be found in Table 2-6.

Table 2-6 gives the percentage of victim/offender relationships derived from three independently generated data sets that cover the same years in Chicago. Because of differences in the way researchers grouped various victim/offender relationships, the categories have been collapsed into three groups for purposes of comparison: offenders known to the victims, strangers, and unknown relationships.

The extent to which information on victim/offender relationships is collected in a similar fashion by different investigators can be determined by comparing the Voss and Hepburn (1968) data and that of Riedel and Zahn (1985) with information provided by the Illinois Criminal Justice Information Authority (ICJIA). The latter frequencies were obtained by collapsing "family" and "acquaintance" homicides for 1965 and 1978.

For 1965, the information on the three categories collected by Voss and Hepburn agrees well with the ICJIA data. For two of three categories, the differences between the two data sets are only one percent while the unknown categories agree exactly. For 1978, the data collected by Riedel and Zahn (1985) agree almost exactly with the ICJIA data concerning stranger homicides; the difference between the two distributions is only 0.3 percent. For the category of offenders known to victims and the unknown category, the difference is approximately 5 percent. Since the Riedel and Zahn category of offenders known to victims is 5 percent higher, and the unknown category is 5 percent lower than the same ICJIA categories, it would appear that we found cases of offenders known to victims that were recorded as unknown when the ICJIA collected their data. Alternatively, our sample may have a slight bias. While the evidence is limited, Table 2-6 suggests that data on victim/offender relationships gathered independently from the same police files agrees well, especially in regard to stranger homicides.

Table 2-6

Comparison of Victim/Offender Relationships for Three Studies of Chicago Homicide

	Voss & Hepburn (1968)	ICJIA*	Riedel & Zahn (1982)	ICJIA
Time period studied	1965	1965	1978	1978
Offender known to victim	77.2%	76.2%	62.8%	57.1%
Stranger	19.0	20.0	21.7	22.0
Unknown	3.8	3.8	15.5	20.9

Total	100.0	100.0	100.0	100.0
Number of Homicides	394	395	425**	790

*Illinois Criminal Justice Information Authority.

**Based on a fifty percent systematic sample.

The Incidence of Stranger Homicides

In order to derive estimates of the incidence of stranger homicides, the research literature was reviewed to find current studies of homicide. The following criteria were used:

1. The time period studied must be 1978 or later.
2. The study must contain a distribution of victim/offender relationships.
3. The victim/offender relationships must be classified into family, friends and acquaintances, and stranger homicides or easily reclassified to fit that trichotomy.
4. It must be a victim-based data set.
5. The data set must consist of homicides reported to the police, rather than offenses at a later stage of criminal justice processing.
6. The data must be gathered from a large city or a county containing the city.
7. Where more than one investigator gathers a data set from the same city, only one data set is used.

Using these criteria, data sets from 10 geographically dispersed cities were used. There were 13 victim/offender relationship distributions because distributions were available from Chicago for each year from 1978 through 1981. The percentage of unknown victim/offender relationships was not available for two studies. The authors, year of publication, research site, time period studied, and victim/offender relationships are given in Table 2-7 on pages 41 and 42.

While the data sets in Table 2-7 are believed to be generally comparable, there are some variations. For example, Wilbanks (1984) used medical examiner records as a primary source, followed by an examination of police records. While he does not indicate to what extent police and medical examiner records agreed, previous research indicates that the agreement is high (Zahn and Riedel, 1983).

In constructing a victim/offender classification from the Wilbanks data set, 550 cases rather than 569 cases were used. Nineteen cases of felons killing police and police killing felons were excluded. Sex partners or rivals and crime partners were included in the friends and acquaintances category. The stranger category also includes cases in which felons killed citizens and citizens killed felons.

In order to get summary measures, the percentages for each of the victim/offender relationship category were ranked, and medians and ranges computed. The results are given in Table 2-8.

Table 2-8 shows that for the 13 victim/offender relationship distributions, the lowest median percent is for homicides involving family members (Mdn = 12.7%). Stranger homicides fall between family and friends and acquaintance homicides with a median of 25.1 percent. Homicides involving friends and acquaintances are the most frequent kind of homicide, with a median percent of 42.3. The median percent of homicides in which the victim/offender relationship is unknown is 20.7.

The ranges for the three victim/offender categories show a substantial amount of variation. This variation has three possible sources. First, cities may differ in the proportion of each of the victim/offender categories involved in homicides. In other words, some cities may have more stranger homicides than others.

Second, there may be classification error by police officers investigating the case. Such classification error could be the result of, for example, inadequate investigation, incorrect reporting, or lack of consensus about the meaning of some types of relationships.

Third, variation in percentages across cities for each of the victim/offender relationships categories may be the result of aggregation error on the part of researchers. For the category of friends and acquaintances, for example, the researchers must aggregate such unclear categories as an unmarried couple sharing a common household, neighbors, employers and employees, customers and proprietors, and divorced couples.

It seems reasonable to suppose that homicides involving family members would present the fewest problems of classification and aggregation of the three victim/offender categories. As was noted earlier, information about the relationship between victim and offender is not only available from offenders who are quickly apprehended, but from neighbors, family members and friends. In addition, for both classification and aggregation purposes, there is a high degree of consensus about the meaning of various types of family relationships. It is, therefore, not surprising that the smallest range (11.3%) in Table 2-8 occurs for homicides involving families.

The comparatively large range for friend and acquaintance homicides (36.8%) presents a different problem. One possibility is that the variation in percentages for this category can be attributed to aggregation error by researchers. Given the wide variety of victim/offender relationships that fall within this category, there may not be a high degree of consensus among researchers on whether neighbors, for example, should be aggregated with friends and acquaintances or strangers.

Table 2-7

Victim/Offender Relationships in
Four Data sets (1978 - 1981)

Data Source	Research Site	Time Period Studied	Number of Cases	Victim/Offender Relation (%)			
				Family	Friends and Acquaint.	Strangers	Unknown
Riedel & Zahn (1985)	Philadelphia	1978	362	12.7	38.1	29.3	19.9
	Newark	1978	102	12.8	31.4	27.4	28.4
	St. Louis	1978	207	13.0	44.4	17.9	24.6
	Memphis	1978	116	13.8	58.6	19.8	7.8
	Dallas	1978	233	18.9	40.8	27.0	13.3
	Oakland	1978	98	11.2	52.0	14.3	22.4
	Ashton	1978	90	21.1	42.2	23.3	13.3

Table 2-7 cont'd

**Victim/Offender Relationships in
Four Data sets (1978 - 1981)**

| Data Source | Research Site | Time Period Studied | Number of Cases | Victim/Offender Relation (%) | | | |
				Family	Friends and Acquaint.	Stranger	Unknown
Illinois C.J. Information Authority	Chicago	1978	790	14.7	42.4	22.0	20.9
		1979	854	11.4	42.3	25.1	21.3
		1980	853	10.9	42.1	26.4	20.6
		1981	87	10.3	36.9	29.6	23.2
Messner & Tardiff (1985)	Manhattan	1981	485	10.5	68.2	21.2	---
Wilbanks (1984)	Dade County (Miami)	1980	569	9.8	60.1	25.7	4.4

Table 2-8

Median and Range of Victim/Offender Relationships
for Thirteen Distributions

Victim/Offender Relationships	Median	Range
Family	12.8	9.8-21.1
Friends and Acquaintances	42.3	31.4-68.2
Strangers	25.1	14.9-29.6
Unknowns	20.7	4.4-28.4

The difficulty with that explanation is that it is not consistent with the results presented in Table 2-6. When the distributions of victim/offender relationships of different studies were compared for the same city and year, classifications among researchers agreed well. In other words, there appears to be a large amount of consensus among researchers when different victim/offender relationships are aggregated. This suggests, in turn, that the percentage of friend and acquaintance homicides varies among cities or that there are classification errors at the level of police investigation that are currently unknown.

The range in the percent of stranger homicides (15.3%) across cities is slightly higher than that found for family homicides, but substantially lower than for friend and acquaintance homicides. There is probably very little aggregation error in this category because data sets normally record only whether there was no prior relationship between victim and offender. Typically, no record is kept of the type of stranger. In other words, the variation in percentages across cities either reflects classification errors by police or variation among cities in the proportion of stranger homicides.

The research by Morgan and Kratcoski (1986) could not be included in Table 2-7 and Table 2-8 because the source of data appears to be court records and because only the percentage of spousal, rather than family, homicides were reported. However, the study does warrant examination. The authors took a 50 percent sample of non-justifiable homicides (N=1,655) in Cuyahoga County (Cleveland) from 1970-1979 to study victim/offender relationships. For the same time period, they collected information on 99 cases of non-justifiable homicide from Tuscaloosa County, Alabama.

Considering only a two-year period, 1978-1979, for the Midwest data, Morgan and Kratcoski found that 48.2 percent of the homicides involved friends and acquaintances and 22.0 percent involved strangers. Because there were only 99 cases for the 10-year period in Tuscaloosa County, the percentages of victim/offender relationships for 1978-1979 are not tabulated. Adding the Cleveland percentages into the distributions given in Table 2-7 does not alter the median percent for family and friend and acquaintance homicides, but it does decrease the median percent of stranger homicides from 25.1 percent to 24.2 percent. While comparisons of the median percents in Table 2-8 to similar median percentages available from the SHR represent comparisons of city to national data, the number and geographical dispersion of the city data suggest national scope. In other words, while comparisons will not result in exact agreement, there should be a pattern of results consistent with what is already known about victim/offender relationships reported by the SHR and city police.

In comparing SHR percentages given in Table 2-1 to those in Table 2-8, only the years from 1978 through 1981 were used; this provides comparability to the years in which data were collected at the city sites. The median for SHR family homicides is 16.8 percent; for friends and acquaintances, it is 36.4 percent; for stranger homicides, the median is 13.4 percent.

While the SHR median for family homicides is higher than that computed on the 13 distributions (12.7%), the difference in medians is the smallest (4.1%) for the three victim/offender relationships. Consistent with results presented in the earlier section, the greatest amount of agreement between police and SHR data was for family homicides.

Also consistent with previously reported research is the intermediate position of friend and acquaintance homicides; the SHR median is 36.4 percent and the 13 distributions median is 42.3 percent, a difference of 5.9 percent. This difference is smaller than that found for friend and acquaintance homicides and larger than for family homicides.

The median percent of stranger homicides reported in Table 2-8 is 25.1 percent. This contrasts with the much smaller median available from SHR percentages: 13.4 percent. The 13 distributions median is 11.7 percent higher than that calculated from SHR percentages, which is consistent with the conclusion that stranger homicides are underreported.

Is Stranger Homicide Increasing?

Because of the underreporting of stranger homicides by the SHR, the nationwide incidence of stranger homicide can only be approximated by examining many studies of homicides in cities. The underreporting of stranger homicides poses an even greater difficulty in trying to ascertain changes because there are few homicide data sets based on city police records that cover more than a few years.

One exception has been the detailed information gathered on 12,872 homicides in Chicago from January, 1965 through December, 1981 and made available through the Illinois Criminal Justice Information Authority. Figure 2-1 constructed from the Chicago data set, shows the changes in victim/offender relationships from 1965-1981.

Figure 2-1 indicates that as an annual proportion of all homicides, those involving strangers increased to 26.6 percent in 1969 from 20.0 percent in 1965, then declined to 15.4 percent in 1977. From 1977 onward the trend was steadily upward to 29.6 percent in 1981. The percentage of stranger homicides for 1981 is the highest in the 17-year period.

Conversely, the trends for family and acquaintance homicides remained the same or declined during the 17-year period. In 1965 and 1967, family homicides were 26.1 percent and 23.4 percent of Chicago homicides; by 1981, family homicides had decreased to 10.3 percent. Likewise, acquaintance homicides showed a decline after reaching a peak in 1973 (49.5%). By 1981, acquaintance homicides were 36.9 percent of all criminal homicides in Chicago.

Figure 2-1 shows a large increase in the number of cases where the type of victim/offender relationship is unknown. In 1965, only 3.8 percent of the victim/offender relationships were unknown; by 1981, this had increased to 23.2 percent.

A major problem in trying to determine whether stranger homicide is increasing by examining city data is whether the results can be generalized. At least concerning total homicides, Block suggests:

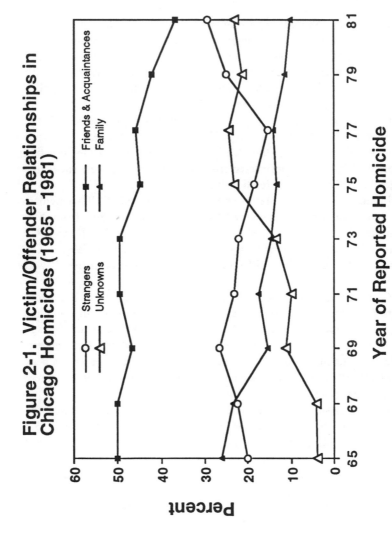

Figure 2-1. Victim/Offender Relationships in Chicago Homicides (1965 - 1981)

Source: Data collected by C. R. Block, R. L. Block, and F. E. Zimring, with the help of the Chicago Police Department

Chicago is not atypical of other large U.S. cities, either in the amount of homicide or in its general pattern over time. Homicide mortality data for total U.S. metropolitan areas show the same rapid increase in the 1960s, a slower increase in the early 1970s, a brief decline, and then another increase. Further, the patterns of change over time in the number of homicides known to the police in two other large northern cities, Philadelphia and Detroit, are similar to the pattern in Chicago. (Block, 1985: 5; Block, 1987: 187-193)

In their study of homicides in Cuyahoga County, Morgan and Kratcoski (1986) found over a 10-year period (1970-1979) that stranger and felony homicides had increased while those involving spouses, relatives, and acquaintances remained the same or declined. Stranger homicides increased from 14.4 percent for the 1970-1971 period to 26.6 percent for the 1972- 1973 period. Stranger homicides declined to 20.3 percent in 1974-1975, then slowly increased to 22.0 percent by 1978-1979. Spouse homicides, by contrast, increased from 14.7 percent in 1970-1971 to 16.4 percent in 1972-1973. From the latter period, spouse homicides decreased to 10.2 percent of all homicides in 1978-1979 (Morgan and Kratcoski, 1986).

A study by Munford, Kazer, Feldman, and Stivers (1976) on 591 Atlanta homicides also provides an indication of changes in the percentage of stranger homicides over time. Munford, et al. analyzed homicides for two time periods (1961-1962, 1971-1972) and divided victim/offender relationships into three groups: relatives and acquaintances, strangers, and unknowns.

In Atlanta, during 1961-1962, stranger homicides represented 1.3 percent of all homicides. By 1971-1972, this percentage had increased to 15.0 percent. While stranger homicides showed an increase, those involving relatives and acquaintances showed a decrease. In 1961-1962, relative and acquaintance homicide accounted for 73.0 percent of the total; by 1971-1972, this had decreased to 71.6 percent.

Unlike the Chicago data, the percentage of unknown relationships in Atlanta declined. In 1961-1962, the percentage unknown was 25.7, but by 1971-1972 this had dropped to 13.4. Another way to determine whether stranger homicides have increased is to look at different studies done at different times in the same city. For Houston, Pokorny's (1965) data on 423 homicide victim/offender relationships were compared to similar data from Lundesgaarde's (1977) study of 200 homicides. Pokorny found that in Houston in 1958-1961, stranger homicides constituted 3.3 percent of the total. Eight years later, in 1969,

Lundesgaarde's research indicated that stranger homicides had increased to 17.5 percent.

Similarly, Wolfgang's (1958) data on 588 homicides in Philadelphia were compared to a distribution of victim/offender relationships available from Riedel and Zahn's (1985) research. Wolfgang found that stranger cases in 1948-1952 made up 12.4 percent of all homicides. By contrast, in 1978, Riedel and Zahn found that stranger homicides were 29.2 percent of all Philadelphia homicides.

Caution must be used in generalizing from the previous limited evidence and postulating a general increase in stranger homicide. First, the only series of data available for more than a few years is limited to two urban areas, Chicago and Cleveland. Second, it is unacceptable to find a trend based on two data points separated by an interval of time; at best, such comparisons indicate a change in the proportion of various types of victim/offender relationships. Such fluctuations may, for example, be the result of changes in the way information is recorded. Third, the risk of error is increased when the two data points are studies done by different researchers at widely varying times in the same city.

Fourth, inferring an increase in the percentage of stranger homicides is risky when the latest data is from 1981. Recently, Silverman and Kennedy (1987) completed a study of stranger homicides in Canada from 1961-1983. They found a dramatic shift in the proportion of stranger homicides from 1980 to 1983. In 1980, the proportion of stranger homicides was 29 percent; for 1982 and 1983, the proportion had declined to 18 percent. There is no assurance that a similar development did not occur in the United States.

Minimally, it can be stated that there is no evidence from studies in United States cities to suggest a decrease in the proportion of homicides involving strangers. Results have been assembled from seven studies in six cities and they uniformly suggest increases. However, there is no general indication of the amount of increase or the stability of increases over time.

Except for the Atlanta study, the proportion of unknown relationships also has increased in the different studies reviewed. Given the greater difficulty experienced by the police in clearing stranger homicides by the arrest of one or more offenders, it is reasonable to suggest that the increase in the proportion of unknown relationships may be because of a larger proportion of stranger homicides.

Are More Robberies Becoming Robbery Homicides?

In addition to knowing whether stranger homicide is increasing, a related question is whether stranger robberies are more often terminating in homicide. Unfortunately, it is difficult to combine victimization and police data to produce a reliable answer. One problem is that stranger homicides tend to be underreported while other forms of violence are reported more often when the offender is a stranger.

Because a large number of robberies involve strangers, an examination of the ratios of robbery murders to robberies would provide some indirect information about whether stranger involvement in violence has been more often terminating in homicide. Cook (1985) studied whether robbery violence had increased by using Return A (see footnote 2) and SHR data from 52 of the nation's largest cities. All the cities had populations in excess of 250,000 people.

In contrast to media accounts that suggest that robberies are becoming more violent, Cook found that "the estimated ratio of robbery murders to robberies shows no consistent increase during the period 1968-1973." (1985: 481). The ratios did increase from 1968 through 1973, remained at about the same level from 1973 through 1979, and then dropped sharply after 1979. While Cook could find no evidence that robberies are, in general, becoming more violent, he suggests that perhaps "a different categorization, for example, focusing on the prior relationships between killer and victim, would exhibit an upward trend during the last decade" (Cook, 1985: 487).

Conclusions

From an examination of the available research on the incidence of stranger violence, the following conclusions seem warranted. First, after a review of the distributions of victim/offender relationships in ten geographically dispersed cities in the United States, it appears that stranger homicides comprise the second highest percentage of homicides. For the ten cities, with data available for one city for four years, the median for stranger homicides was 25.1 percent. The analysis suggests that stranger homicides may range over cities from about 14 percent to about 30 percent.

Homicides involving friends and acquaintances comprise the largest percentage of the total number of homicides. The median for the fourteen distributions was 42.3 percent with a range from 31.4 percent to 68.2 percent.

The smallest proportion was for homicides involving family members. The median percent for this category was 12.7 percent with a range of from 9.8 percent to 21.1 percent.

Second, comparison with nationwide SHR percentages for the years 1978-1981 indicates results consistent with patterns reported in earlier sections. While family homicides tended to be overreported, the difference between the SHR median percentage and that found in the fourteen distributions was the smallest (4.1%). Friend and acquaintance homicides tended to be underreported with a somewhat larger difference between the medians (5.9%). The largest difference between the percentages reported by SHR and those available from the fourteen distributions was for stranger homicides. While the SHR reports a median of 13.4 percent for the four years, the median percent of stranger homicides for the fourteen distributions is 25.1 percent, a difference of 11.7 percent.

Third, an examination of previous research to determine whether stranger violence has increased is suggestive, particularly concerning stranger homicides. A seventeen-year series of homicide data from Chicago, a ten-year series from Cleveland, comparison of two time periods separated by a decade in Atlanta, and comparisons of four studies done at different times in Houston and Philadelphia, indicate an increase in stranger homicides.

The likelihood of an increase in stranger homicides is given further support by an increase in most studies of homicides with unknown relationships. Since stranger homicides are more difficult to clear by arrest, an increase in homicides of unknown relationships might be due, in part, to an increase in stranger homicides. The conclusions rests, however, on a tenuous empirical basis in which the most appropriate conclusion is that there is no evidence that stranger homicides have decreased.

Fourth, that robberies, rapes, and assaults are increasingly resulting in lethal outcomes was disputed by the results of Cook's research. Cook examined the ratio of robbery murders to robberies for the period 1968-1973 and suggested that there is no evidence that robberies are becoming more violent. There has been no research to determine whether this conclusion is applicable to stranger robbery.

Fifth, it should be kept in mind that the estimates and ranges for victim/offender relationships in homicide are approximations and subject to unknown amounts of error. There is a presumption in this analysis that police records are a more accurate source of information about stranger related homicide than SHR data. While the problems of classification and underreporting have been discussed with respect to the SHR, there is little information about the reliability of police record classifications. The evaluation of the variation in the ranges reported suggests that classification errors may play an important role, particularly with the percentage of friends and acquaintances, and stranger homicides.

Finally, there is a considerable uncertainty in suggesting that the best approximation of the incidence of stranger homicides is 25 percent. Quite aside from the methodological problems, it should be remembered that for the most recent study reviewed, data was collected in 1981. While this is more relevant in discussions of whether stranger homicides are increasing, it is a reminder that more recent information is not available.

NOTES

1. The NCHS uses a broader definition of homicide than the UCR program. The former classify their mortality data using periodic revisions of the International Classification of Diseases (1977). Homicide as an "external cause" of death consists of the following twelve categories:

    1. Late effect of injury purposely inflicted by another person, except in war.

    2. Nonaccidental poisoning.

    3. Corrosive or caustic substances.

    4. Firearms and explosives.

    5. Cutting and piercing instruments.

    6. Fight, brawl, or rape.

    7. Hanging and strangulation.

    8. Drowning.

    9. Child battering and other maltreatment.

    10. Other and unspecified means.

    11. Injury by intervention by police.

    12. Executions.

2. According to the UCR, criminal homicide is divided into murder and nonnegligent manslaughter, which is defined as the "willful (nonnegligent) killing of one human being by another." (UCR Handbook, 1980) As a general rule, any death due to injuries received in a fight, argument, quarrel, assault, or commission of a crime is counted as a murder or nonnegligent manslaughter.

Suicides, accidental deaths, assaults to murder, attempted murders, and justifiable and excusable homicides are not included in the category of murder and nonnegligent manslaughter. Manslaughter by negligence involves the killing of another person through negligence. Traffic fatalities are excluded.

3. The four sources of data are:

1. Return A - Monthly Return of Offenses Known to the Police. All offenses, including murder and nonnegligent manslaughter, are reported to the police on this form.

2. UCR Estimates. Estimates based on Return A which correct for underreporting.

3. Supplementary Homicide Reports. This form requests detailed data on the victim, offender, circumstances and victim/offender relationship.

4. Age, Sex, and Race of Arrest Offenders. This form requests aggregated monthly data on the age, sex, and race of arrested offenders. (Uniform Crime Reporting Handbook, 1981)

4. The police and the UCR routinely collect information on victim/offender relationships using very specific designations. The UCR-SHR form, for example, has thirty-one different categories for various types of victim/offender relationships. There is only one category for stranger relationships, however. In the research reported here, reduction of police generated categories to three or four broad types of relationship is commonly done. The four categories are: (1) within family, (2) friends and acquaintances, (3) strangers, (4) unknown.

5. The author acknowledges the help of E. Winslow Chapman, former Director of Police Services of the Memphis Police Department, who implemented the HEIDI project. The HEIDI instrument and adaptation to SPSS analysis was developed by Dr. Fred Klyman. The data is used with permission.

6.   The author would like to thank Carolyn Rebecca Block, Illinois
     Criminal Justice Information Authority; Richard Block, Loyola
     University; and Franklin Zimring, now at the University of
     California, Berkeley, for making available data on homicide
     victim/offender relationships in Chicago for 1965 - 1981. Results
     presented here will differ from those found in Block (1976, 1977)
     because this analysis treated unknown relationships as a separate
     category.

REFERENCES

Block, C. R. (1987). Homicide in Chicago. Chicago: Center for Urban Policy, Loyola University of Chicago.

Block, C. R. (1985). Lethal violence in Chicago over seventeen years: Homicides known to the police, 1965-1981. Chicago: Statistical Analysis Center, Illinois Criminal Justice Information Authority.

Block, R. (1976). Homicide in Chicago - A nine year study (1965-1973). Journal of Criminal Law and Criminology, 66, 496-510.

Block, R. (1977). Violent crime: Environment, interaction and death. Lexington: Lexington Books.

Cantor, D. & Cohen, L. E. (1980). Comparing measures of homicide trends: Methodological and substantive differences in the vital statistics and Uniform Crime Report time series (1933- 1975). Social Science Research, 9, 121-145.

Cook, P. J. (1985). Is robbery becoming more violent? An analysis of robbery murder trends since 1968. Journal of Criminal Law and Criminology, 76, 480-489.

Federal Bureau of Investigation (Annual editions, 1976-1983). Uniform crime reports. Washington: U. S. Government Printing Office.

Federal Bureau of Investigation (1980). Uniform crime reporting handbook. Washington: U. S. Government Printing Office.

Federal Bureau of Investigation (1981). Uniform crime reporting handbook. Washington: U.S. Government Printing Office.

Loftin, C., Kindley, K., Norris, S. L. & Wiersema, B. (1987). An attribute approach to relationships between offenders and victims. Journal of Criminal Law and Criminology, 78, 259-271.

Lundsgaarde, H. F. (1977). Murder in space city: A cultural analysis of Houston homicide patterns. New York: Oxford University Press.

Memphis Police Department. Instruction manual for homicide enforcement investigation index (HEIDI), unpublished, no date.

Messner, S. F. & Tardiff, K. (1986). The social ecology of urban homicide: An application of the "routine activities" approach. Criminology, 23, 241-267.

Morgan, F. & Kratcoski, P. C. (1986). An analysis of the victim-offender relationship in homicide cases. Journal of Police and Criminal Psychology, 2, 52-63.

Munford, R. S., Kazer, R. S., Feldman, R. A. & Stivers, R. R. (1976). Homicide trends in Atlanta. Criminology, 14, 213-231.

National Center for Health Statistics (1977). International classification of diseases. Washington: U. S. Government Printing Office.

Pokorny, A. D. (1965). A comparison of homicide in two cities. Journal of Criminal Law, Criminology, and Police Science, 56, 479-487.

Riedel, M. (November, 1981). Stranger homicides in an American city. Paper presented at the meeting of the American Society of Criminology, Washington.

Riedel, M. & Zahn, M. (1985). The nature and patterns of American homicide. Washington: U.S. Government Printing Office.

Riedel, M. (1987). Stranger violence: Perspectives, issues, and problems. Journal of Criminal Law and Criminology, 78, 223-258.

Riedel, M. (1990). Nationwide homicide data sets: An evaluation of Uniform Crime Reports and National Center for Health Statistics data. In D. L. MacKenzie, P. J. Baunach, and R. Roberg (Eds.), Measuring crime: Large-scale, long-range efforts. (pp. 175-205). Albany: SUNY Press.

Sellin, T. (1962). The significance of records of crime. In M. E. Wolfgang, L. Savitz and N. Johnson (Eds.), The sociology of crime and delinquency. (pp. 59-68). New York: John Wiley.

Silverman, R. A. & Kennedy, L. W. (1987). Relational distance and homicide: The role of the stranger. Journal of Criminal Law and Criminology, 78, 272-308.

Voss, H. L. & Hepburn, J. R. (1968). Patterns in criminal homicides in Chicago. Journal of Criminal Law, Criminology, and Police Science, 59, 500-508.

Wilbanks, W. (1984). Murder in Miami: An analysis of homicide patterns and trends in Dade County (Miami) Florida, 1917-1988. Lanham, MD: University Press of America.

Williams, K. & Flewelling, R. L. (1987). Family, acquaintance, and stranger homicide: Alternative procedures for rate calculations. Criminology, 25, 543-560.

Wolfgang, M. E. (1958). Patterns in criminal homicide. Philadelphia: University of Pennsylvania Press.

Zahn, M. A. & Riedel, M. (1983). National versus local data sources in the study of homicide: Do they agree? In G. P. Waldo (Ed.), Measurement in criminal justice. (pp. 103-120). Beverly Hills: Sage Publications.

Zahn, M. A. & Sagi, P. C. (1987). Stranger homicides in nine American cities. Journal of Criminal Law and Criminology, 78, 377-397.

Zimring, F. E. & Zuehl, J. (1986). Victim injury and death in urban robbery: A Chicago study. Journal of Legal Studies, 15, 1-40.

CHAPTER 3

NON-FATAL STRANGER VIOLENCE

This chapter examines and evaluates research on the incidence and trends of non-fatal forms of stranger violence. Unlike homicides, the Uniform Crime Reporting Program provides information only on the total number of robberies, assaults and rapes and aggregated monthly data on the age, sex, and race of arrested offenders. The sole national source of information on non-fatal stranger violence is the National Crime Survey (NCS). Following an introduction to the NCS, the available research on amounts and changes in non-fatal stranger violence will be presented. The remainder of the chapter will discuss the problems in measuring stranger involvement in robberies, assaults, and rapes, and the difficulties in comparing results from the NCS with those from the Uniform Crime Reporting Program.

Measuring Non-Fatal Forms of Stranger Violence

Recording the incidence of non-fatal forms of stranger violence presents different kinds of problems than recording the incidence of stranger homicide. If the allocation of resources for measuring the phenomena is an indication of their severity, then homicides are obviously more serious offenses than robberies, assaults, and rapes. As indicated in the previous chapter, there are two national and local agencies that collect data on the same homicide phenomena. Until the emergence of the NCS in the mid-sixties, only minimal amounts of information were available from the police for robberies, assaults, and rapes. Unlike homicide, the victim of other forms of stranger violence can choose to conceal the existence of the offense from the police unless it is observed by them or other witnesses. Thus, while the unexplained absence of another person, suggesting the possibility of homicide, stimulates inquiries by others, the occurrence of a stranger robbery, assault, or rape may be known only to the victim and the offender.

The negative physical, psychological and social consequences of stranger violence do not lead to greater emphasis on it by law enforcement agencies. There is relatively little data available on non-fatal stranger violence from the Uniform Crime Reporting Program. Interpersonal violence often has very traumatic effects on the victim. In their study of mugging victims, Lejeune and Alex (1973), for example, found that many of them underwent a "vulnerability conversion" after the mugging. Before the violent encounter, the respondents had believed their immediate everyday environment was safe and that violent victimization happened to other people. "But uniformly, and without exception in our sample, one effect of the mugging is to raise to a significant degree the victim's sense of vulnerability and mistrust." (LeJeune and Alex, 1973: 272) When asked whether the mugging experience had changed their outlook on life, one respondent said:

> Oh, for months I was in terror. Even now I never turn to the door without making sure that I turn around. And for about six months I paid a monthly fee to my super [to act as a bodyguard]. It was a horrible feeling of terror that followed me. And I'm not usually the most fearful person. Nobody's a hero, but I went everywhere and did all kinds of things. I went out evenings. Now I don't go out evenings at all. I'm like a prisoner here in the evening. I'm really afraid. This is the tragedy of my life....(pp. 274-275)

Police generated statistics on non-fatal stranger violence do not provide information needed by researchers because the statistics reflect the organizational goal of law enforcement: investigation and apprehension of offenders. The creation of police statistics occurs in the course of implementing this goal, which is primarily concerned with offenders. In other words, criminal justice statistics, including police statistics, can be used as a source of information by researchers, but that is not the major reason for their existence (Sparks, 1982). As Gove, Hughes, and Geerken (1985) have indicated in their comparison of the NCS and the Uniform Crime Reporting Program, victims report a crime to the police with the expectation that something will be done. Or, if nothing else, the report will support their insurance claim.

By the late 1960s, it was clear from the writings of von Hentig (1948), Mendelsohn (1963), and Wolfgang (1958) that the victim was a causal factor in the occurrence of crime. For a better understanding of crime, there was an obvious need to develop sources of information about the characteristics of the victim and the nature of his or her interaction with the offender. In addition, there was a growing recognition of the deficiencies and biases of the Uniform Crime Reporting Program. Disenchantment with these police-based statistics grew out of several years of extensive critiques and criticisms (Beattie, 1962; Lejins, 1966; Robison, 1966; Sellin, 1962; Wolfgang, 1963). It was the creation of the President's Commission on Law Enforcement and the Administration of Justice in 1965 that provided the opportunity for a victimization survey. The initial such survey was conducted by Albert D. Biderman in Washington, D.C. The study used interviews from 511 randomly selected adults in three police districts.

Two other surveys were conducted during this early period, one by Albert J. Reiss, Jr. and the other by Philip H. Ennis. The Reiss survey focused on criminal victimization of businesses and organizations while the Ennis survey was a national probability sample (Sparks, 1982).

The National Crime Survey went through many changes after the three surveys were done (Lehnen and Skogan, 1981). The three surveys were, however, "undoubtedly landmarks in the study of crime. Between them, they uncovered almost all of the methodological problems inherent in victimization surveying. They also produced major substantive findings that would be confirmed by most, if not all, later surveys" (Sparks, 1982: 45).

The problems involving police statistics that victimization surveys were meant to address can be illustrated by considering Figure 3-1. In step 1, the crime must be perceived by someone other than the offender, it may be a victim, a bystander, or a police officer. The eyewitness must define the act as a crime (Step 2); he or she must conclude that the act is not an accident, mistake, joke or pretense. Unless the person observing it is a police officer, the act must be reported (Step 3). If the act is reported, then the police can redefine it (Step 4); in other words, the police may or may not regard the act as a crime. Finally, if the police do regard the act as a crime, then it must be recorded (Step 5). Obviously, if a crime is to be reported, all the preceding steps must be followed.

Most of the shortcomings with this procedure manifest themselves at the third step in Figure 3-1. Crimes are not reported to the police in

Figure 3-1

Processes Involved in the Construction of Police Statistics of
"Crimes Known"*

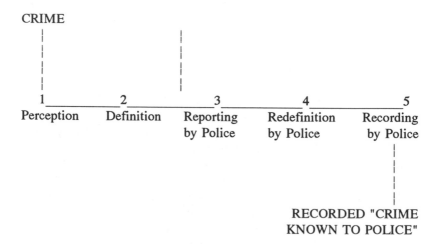

CRIME

1	2	3	4	5
Perception	Definition	Reporting by Police	Redefinition by Police	Recording by Police

RECORDED "CRIME
KNOWN TO POLICE"

*Taken from Sparks (1982: 14).

large numbers and for a variety of reasons. Once reported, they are
ignored, defined out of existence or not recorded by the police. The
obvious solution is to measure the amount of crime without relying on
police intervention and at a point closest to the event. This occurs
between the second and third step, indicated by a downward pointing line
in Figure 3-1.

What made the use of victimization surveys an even more attractive
means for uncovering the "dark number" of crimes was that the
methodology needed was highly developed and had been used in similar
contexts. Survey methodology had been employed as early as 1920 to
learn about people's spending habits, attitudes, incomes, and voting
intentions. Nor was asking people about their experience with crime a
novel use of survey methods; as Sparks (1982) indicates, self-reported
crime and delinquency studies have been around for two decades by
1965. The question was not whether survey methodology could be used
to measure the amount of victimization, but why it had not been used
sooner.

Victimization surveys sought to create a data source that did not suffer from the biases and deficiencies of police statistics. After more than twenty years of experience with the National Crime Survey, however, it has become apparent that some of the problems in measuring crime are endemic. A major outcome of efforts to measure victimization has been an increased general awareness by criminologists that the measurement and reporting of crime is subject to a large number of psychological, social, and organizational variables which constrain and limit what is reported. Thus, while the specific problems are different for police-based statistics in comparison with victimization surveys, serious issues of measurement remain. Before considering these issues and how they affect the measurement of stranger violence, a review of the research on incidence and trends is necessary.

Changes in Non-Fatal Forms of Stranger Violence

A 1987 report of the Bureau of Justice Statistics describes the incidence and characteristics of violent crime, excluding homicides, for different victim/offender relationships. The data were drawn from the 1982-1984 National Crime Survey and consisted of an average sample of 58,000 households and 123,000 people; the latter were interviewed twice a year. Series crimes, those in which there were three or more incidents about which the victim could not provide details on separate events, were included in the counts as one incident.

Three victim/offender relationship categories were used. Crimes committed by relatives included spouses and ex-spouses, parents, children, siblings and other relatives as victims. The category of acquaintance included casual acquaintances, friends, boyfriends, girlfriends, and other non-related but well-known persons. Strangers were divided into those people completely unknown and those known only by sight. Offenders were known 'by sight only' if the victim never said more than hello to the offender" (1987: 1).

According to the victimization surveys, strangers have a pronounced involvement in violent crimes. For the 1982-1984 period, 57 percent of the victimizations for rape, robbery, and assaults were committed by strangers; 46 percent by offenders completely unknown and 11 percent by persons known only by sight.

Thirty-one percent of the violent victimizations involved acquaintances. The single largest category (14%) was for casual acquaintances, followed by non-related but well-known persons (6%), and friends/ex-friends (6%). The categories of girlfriends, boyfriends were less than 4 percent.

According to the victimization survey, relatives made up only eight percent of the violent victimizations. In three percent of the victimizations, the relationship could not be ascertained.

Robbery was the offense most often committed by strangers; 77 percent of the robbery victimizations were committed by strangers. The percentages of stranger involvement for rape (55%), aggravated assault (56%), and simple assault (52%) were very similar.

Violent victimizations involving acquaintances were higher in simple assault (36%), rape (35%), and aggravated assault (30%) than in robbery (15%). Relatives made up less than ten percent of the victimizations for any one of the violent crimes used in this survey.

Inferences about trends in non-fatal forms of stranger violence are even more tenuous than those for stranger homicides. About all that can be done with the national surveys is a comparison of the results of the 1982-1984 survey with those of the 1973-1979 survey. Between 1982 and 1984, 57 percent of the victimizations reported to the National Crime Survey involved strangers (Bureau of Justice Statistics, 1987). In the years 1973-1979, 59 percent of all violent victimizations, excluding homicide, involved strangers (Bureau of Justice Statistics, 1982). Thus, results from the two National Crime Survey reports suggest that stranger involvement in rape, robbery, and assault have generally remained stable.

For the two time periods covered by the reports, the percentage of stranger rapes declined. In the 1973-1979 period, stranger rapes were 65 percent of violent victimizations; in 1982-1984, they were 55 percent.

Robbery, aggravated assault, and simple assault changed very little between the two periods. Robbery-stranger victimizations increased from 76 percent to 77 percent, aggravated assault remained the same (56%), and simple assault decreased from 53 percent to 52 percent.

It was estimated previously that at least 25 percent of the homicides in large urban areas involves strangers. In view of this low, albeit conservative estimate, the finding that 57 percent of robberies, assaults, and rapes involve strangers seems surprising. Paradoxically, while the preceding chapter provided evidence that police departments report too few stranger homicides, the research on the NCS reviewed in the following section suggests that it reports too few nonstranger robberies, assaults and rapes.

THE NATIONAL CRIME SURVEY AND STRANGER VIOLENCE

It is an assumption of the NCS that the best "statistical results are to be expected . . . when data are gathered for their own sake, rather than as an appendage to some other administrative procedure." (Petersen, 1975: 49) The results of more than twenty years' use of the NCS have contributed an impressive amount to our understanding of crime and criminal victimization. The NCS results show that only a small proportion of crime that occurs is reported to the police. For example, the National Opinion Research Center (NORC) conducted by Ennis on a national probability sample of 9,644 households found that the estimated robbery rate was 94.0 per 100,000. The rate calculated from Uniform Crime Reporting Program data was 61.4 per 100,000. For aggravated assault, the NORC rate was more than twice as high (218.3) as that available from police-based statistics (106.6). The estimated forcible rape rate (42.5) was nearly four times higher than that available from Uniform Crime Reporting Program data (11.6) (Ennis, 1967a, 1967b).

The NCS also has provided a wealth of information about the incidence, distribution, and characteristics of crime and victims of crime (Sparks, 1982). The NCS has provided information on violent crime rates, rates for age, gender, ethnic and racial groups, single and multiple victimizations, and how these cultural and demographic categories are related to each other and to variables like location, income, and attitudes.

Such an outpouring of information has stimulated the development of theory to assimilate, organize, and explain these results. Theoretical developments include the useful classification by Sparks (1982) of the ways in which victims can contribute to their own victimization. On a larger scale, Hindelang, Gottfredson, and Garofalo (1978) have proposed a lifestyle theory to explain violent victimization. The NCS is, however, not without major methodological deficiencies, particularly concerning the measurement of stranger violence. Indeed, as will be seen, so extensive are these difficulties that one group of authors has suggested that the Uniform Crime Reporting Program continues to provide more valid information on serious crimes (Gove, et al., 1985). Figure 3-2 is useful as a beginning point to examine some of the problems involved in measuring stranger violence from the perspective of the process used to construct survey estimates.

Step 1 and step 2 are similar to the processes that occur in police statistics and need no further discussion. Step 7 and step 8 refer to practices and standards of good survey practice. The variety of complex statistical questions that emerge at step 9 are related to the sampling process (step 3). Most of the problems that are found in victimization studies, including the measurement of stranger violence, occur in steps 4 through 6.

Validating the Measurement of Stranger Violence

The NCS relies on the victim to determine whether a crime has occurred. By contrast, police statistics rely on the judgment of police officers. In addition, for police statistics, a police officer is present at or near the time of the offense and can redefine the information provided by the victim. The NCS does not have the advantage of an additional outside observer; it must rely on the victim's definition of the event six months to a year after it occurred. Thus, there are problems of recall in victimization surveys and questions about the extent to which what is recalled reflects accurately what originally happened.

One approach to validating the NCS has used police reports of the original event. "Reverse record check" validation studies select a sample of police records for a specific jurisdiction and period of time. Using this information, the victims are interviewed to determine the extent to which the reported incident is recalled.

From the viewpoint of measuring stranger violence, one of the most important "reverse record check" studies was done by Turner (1981) in San Jose. The major purpose of the San Jose study was to examine the memory bias in the recall of victimization incidents.

A probability sample of 620 violent crime reports was selected from the files of the San Jose City Police Department. Personal rather than commercial victims were chosen to provide uniform representation over each of the twelve months of 1970. There was uniform representation for each of the following offenses: robbery, assault, burglary, rape, and larceny. Except for rape, twelve offense reports were chosen for each month; for rape, six offense reports were used for each month.

Figure 3-2

Processes Involved in the Construction of Survey Estimates of
Criminal Victimization*

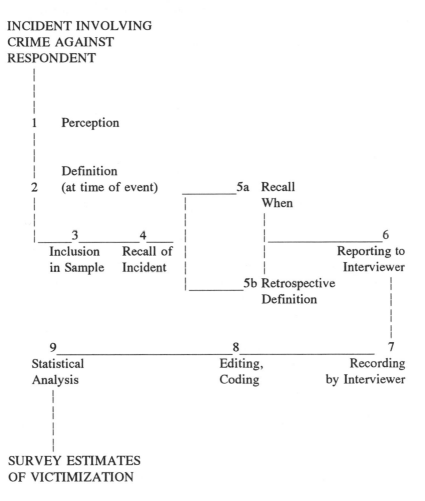

Taken from Sparks (1982: 66)

The interview team succeeded in interviewing 394 persons, 63.5 percent of the original 620 victims. Of those not interviewed, 76 percent could not be located, 11 percent had moved, and 13 percent were not interviewed for other reasons, including refusals.

Table 3-1 compares victim-offenders relationships by whether the incident was reported in the interview. Only the violent offenses of robbery, assault, and rape are used in the tabulations.

Slightly over three-fourths (76.3%) of the violent stranger incidents reported to the police were recalled by respondents. This contrasts with about half (56.9%) of the incidents involving known offenders, excluding relatives. Less than one-fourth (22.2%) of the incidents in which a relative was the offender were recalled by the respondents.

More detailed examination of Table 3-1 shows that a major difference exists in the recall of assaults involving strangers and relatives. While 54.2 percent of the assaults in which a stranger was the offender were reported on the victimization survey, only 22.2 percent of the assaults in which a relative was the offender were recalled. In contrast, assaults in which the offender was known to the victim were more often recalled (81.6%) than assaults in which the offender was a stranger (54.2%).

Table 3-1 also demonstrates that rapes and robberies with stranger offenders were more likely to be recalled on the victimization survey than the same offenses in which the offender was known to the victim. Eighty-four percent of the rapes and 80.4 percent of the robberies involving strangers were recalled by the respondent. By comparison, 54.2 percent of the rapes and 68.9 percent of the robberies were recalled when the offender was known to the respondent-victim.

To provide further evidence that assaults involving relatives are underreported, Turner (1981) gave a breakdown by victim/offender relationships of the total number of incidents not reported in the interview. Using weighted percentages, 63 percent involved offenders known to the victim and 31 percent were incidents in which the offender was a stranger. Six percent of the victim/offender relationships was not recorded. Thus, violent offenses involving relatives and other persons known to the victim were reported in victimization surveys much less often than incidents involving strangers.

There is one other methodological alternative for the differences in reporting of victim/offender relationships between police and victimization

Table 3-1

Police Sample Cases Interviewed by Victim/Offender Relationship,
by Whether Incident was Reported in Interview**

Victim/offender relationship and reporting status	Assault	Rape	Robbery	Total	Total weighted (percent)*
Total cases	81	45	80	206	
Proportion reporting incident (percent)	48.1	66.7	76.3	63.1	63.7
Offender a relative	18			18	
Proportion reporting incident (percent)	22.2			22.2	22.2
Offender known	38	24	16	78	
Proportion reporting incident (percent)	81.6	54.2	68.9	57.7	56.9
Offender a stranger	24	19	56	99	
Proportion reporting incident (percent)	54.2	84.2	80.4	74.7	76.3
No entry for offender	1	2	8	11	
Proportion reporting incident (percent)	100.0	50.0	62.5	63.6	61.5

*   Recomputed to adjust for differential expected sample size by type of crime - size of sample for rape was N/2; for robbery and assault, the sample size was each n.

**   Taken from Turner (1981: 26)

surveys. In the reverse record check research, a pool of offenses was selected and the victims interviewed. An alternative to this method is to select a number of incidents and victims from the survey and determine to what extent they can be found in police files. This "forward record check" can be used to determine whether the type of victim/offender relationship was reported accurately on the victimization survey.

Schneider (1981) did a forward record check of incidents reported to interviewers in 1974 during a victimization survey of Portland, Oregon. She matched the incidents reported in the interviews with information found in police files. A "definite match" was secured for 45 percent of the 476 incidents recorded. A definite match was one in which there was at least 90 percent agreement on victim/household characteristics between the survey and the police data. Although the percentage of matches is low, Schneider indicates that about the same percentage of incidents involving strangers and nonstrangers are reported on the interview.

In 13, or 52 percent, of the 25 cases involving offenders known to the victim, the victim provides the same information about victim/offender relationships to the police and the NCS interviewer. In 25, or 58 percent, of the 43 cases involving strangers, the victims report the same information to the police and the interviewer. Victims, Schneider concluded, appear not to fail intentionally to tell the interviewer whether they knew the offender. Schneider's research also suggests that there is slightly better agreement between survey and police data for incidents involving strangers.

Comparing Schneider's (1981) and Turner's (1981) research to the earlier NCS report (Bureau of Justice Statistics, 1987), it appears that stranger violence may not be overreported with respect to their frequency, but they are substantially overreported with respect to percentages. Thus, it was indicated in the previous section that 57 percent of the violent incidents reported in the NCS involved strangers. What is inflating this percentage is not the overreporting of stranger incidents by victims, but the underreporting of violent incidents involving relatives. Because the percentage of specific types of victim/offender relationships is based on the total number of incidents, a small percentage of incidents in which the offender is a relative will automatically mean a much larger percentage of violent incidents in which the offender is a stranger.

Is Nonstranger Violence Underreported?

Studies using reverse record checks assume for research purposes that all incidents have been reported to the police. But does the reporting of violent incidents to the police vary by victim/offender relationships? If, for example, assaults involving relatives are less often reported to the police than stranger assaults, then the underreporting in police statistics, added to that noted in reverse record check studies, would suggest that estimates derived from victimization surveys would be biased by a very large, albeit unknown, amount.

Block (1974) used data on 190 assaults from the NORC study done in 1967 to test this idea. Of the 190 assaults, 56 percent were reported to the police. He notes that this is a higher percentage of police notification than the 49 percent that occurred for the survey as a whole.

Block found support for his hypothesis that the closer the relationship between victim and assailant, the less likely it is that the police will be notified. Of 34 assault incidents involving strangers, 66 percent included notification of the police. By contrast, for 83 assault incidents in which the offender was known, but not a relative, 51 percent were reported to the police. Finally, among 64 incidents in which a relative was the offender, only 44 percent were reported.

Block (1974) used the victim/offender relationship variable, a measure of victim's involvement in the assault, race, and income in a further analysis and concluded:

Nothing presented in this paper is really unexpected. Variables which should rationally go into the victim's decision to notify the police of an attack are, in fact, related to the victim's decision. The closer the relationship of victim and assailant the less likely notification will be. The greater the implication of the victim, the less likely he will notify the police. The higher the victim's social class the less likely will be notification. (p. 568)

Skogan (1976) has also explored the effect of victim/offender relationships on reporting. He pooled six monthly random victimization survey samples of the American population done from July to December of 1973. Unlike the Block research, these surveys were "bounded" by earlier interviews to prevent respondents from attributing incidents to one survey period that properly belonged in an earlier period. The data also were subjected to "an extensive series of methodological and validity checks" that may not have been used in the 1967 NORC sample (Skogan, 1976: 538).

In general, crimes involving strangers were more often reported than crimes in which the victim was known to the offender, although the differences were small. For stranger crimes against the person, assaults, assaultive violence, and assaultive violence without theft, the percent reported to the police ranged from 41.4 percent to 44.8 percent. For the same crimes, about 38 of the victims who knew their offender notified the police. Thus, the difference between police notification for stranger and nonstranger incidents was about 4 percent.

For rape, 47.8 percent of the stranger incidents led to notification of the police in comparison with 30.9 percent of the incidents in which the victim was known to the offender. Stranger assaultive violence with theft prompted the highest percentage of notifications. Sixty-four percent of the stranger incidents and 48.7 percent of the nonstranger incidents were reported to the police.

Skogan concluded that reporting incidents to the police was only weakly related to victim characteristics. However, characteristics of the victim's experience, such as the value of the stolen or damaged property, the amount of injury, the use of a weapon, and the extent to which the crime intruded into the private lifespace of the victim were highly evocative of police notification. "Attributes of their experiential world rather than social or symbolic forces appear to motivate the victims of crime, suggesting that the decision to report may be a highly cognitive, reality-testing process" (p. 548).

As a final bit of evidence, Skogan examined for each of six offenses the percentage of nonreporting respondents who indicated they did not notify the police because "nothing could be done." This distribution was compared to the percentage of offenses cleared, as reported by the FBI. The lowest percentages of those saying "nothing could be done" were for crimes that were high in clearances, such as assaults. On the other hand, the highest percentages of those saying "nothing could be done" were for offenses with the lowest clearance values. The simplest interpretation, Skogan suggests, "is that people do not report when they think nothing will happen as a result, and . . . they are often right" (1976: 549).

The research by Skogan (1976) and Block (1974) suggests that violent incidents in which the offender is known or is a close relative are less likely to be reported to the police than stranger incidents. However, the two researchers differ in the importance they assign to victim/offender relationships in the notification decision.

Gove, et al. (1985) provides additional evidence to support the view that assaults involving nonstrangers are underreported to the police. They suggest that in assaults where the offender and victim know one another, the police generally make a serious effort to reconcile the two parties, thereby avoiding any official action (Berk, Loseke, Berk, and Rauma, 1980; Berk and Loseke, 1981; Gottfredson and Gottfredson, 1988). The consequent underreporting of assaults means that the pool of police offenses used by reverse record check studies is one in which many nonstranger assaults are not included. This suggests that the underreporting of nonstranger assaults in victimization surveys is much larger than reported in reverse record check research.

Further, Skogan notes that NCS reports on victimization by acquaintances and relatives does not correspond with what is known about interpersonal violence:

> The evidence from other sources is that a much higher proportion of assaults, and even rapes, takes place within friendship and family circles. Numerous studies of police homicide files suggest that strangers account for only about 25 percent of all urban murders. Homicide and assault are similar in origin and process, differing primarily in their outcome--which is often a function of such factors as the caliber of gun employed or the availability of a doctor (Zimring, 1972). Curtis' (1974) survey of official records in 17 major cities found that only 21 percent of all assaults in 1966 were attributed by investigating officers to strangers. These proportions are similar to those revealed in numerous crime-specific studies of police file data. They render the survey data even more suspect because we believe that violence between friends and relatives is less likely than stranger violence to be reported to the police. That police files contain approximately 3 1/2 times more acquaintance violence than revealed in interviews does not add to our confidence in the validity of survey findings. (Skogan, 1982: 30)

In contrast to reports to the police, respondents on victimization surveys have the opportunity to engage in what Sparks (1982) called "retrospective definition." An event may have been perceived, defined, and reported as a crime at the time of its occurrence, but after the passage of some months, the same event may not be defined and reported to the NCS interviewer as a crime by its victim (see Figure 3-2). It is suggested here that this process differs by victim/offender relationship.

In her study of the disputing process among Rock Island fisherman, Yngvesson (1978) found that whether a grievance was handled formally or informally depended on the relationship between the grieving parties. A serious disagreement between a community member and a stranger-outsider was more likely to be handled by formal legal means while one involving community members was more likely to be settled informally.

Yngvesson suggested that the community has less of a social investment and interest in the behavior of the stranger. Further, the aggrieved party does not have to be concerned about the effect of grievance on later relationships, an important consideration for community members. On the other hand, what happens to the stranger after the event probably will have little impact on the grievant or the community.

A similar logic applies to victims of violence. Where the offender is a stranger, the definition of the act at the time of the event is not subject to restructuring because the victim and offender are not likely to have any further interaction. Thus, at the time of the interview survey, the stranger incident continues to be defined in the same way. On the other hand, where the offender and victim are relatives, their interaction is very likely to continue beyond the time of the incident. Given this additional time period, it is likely that the event is discussed and reevaluated by the victim, his family and the offender. Other members of the family may encourage a non-criminal definition. "[A]ssaults typically arise over very trivial matters (Mulville, Tumin, and Curtis, 1967; Curtis, 1974) and when one has a close relationship with an individual one tends, over time, to put the assault into the context of one's overall relationship with the person and as a consequence the incident tends to become normalized" (Gove, et al., 1985: 486). Once the original event is retrospectively defined as something other than a crime, it is not likely that it will be reported on a victimization survey.

The inability to obtain an accurate report of non-fatal violence involving nonstrangers makes it difficult to provide a meaure of non-fatal stranger violence. As noted earlier, simple comparisons between stranger violence and other victim/offender relationships are distorted by the underreporting of violence involving known offenders, particularly relatives. In short, from reviewing the victimization literature, it is not possible to provide a comparative figure indicating the amount of non-fatal stranger violence.

While there are difficulties with using rates with survey data, it is possible to develop rates of non-fatal stranger violence. Such rates would use an estimate of the population at risk as a denominator, thus freeing the measure of stranger violence from the problem of proportions and percentages. Non-fatal stranger violence rates could be used to compare changes in the amount of violence over time in the same jurisdiction.

If a measure of non-fatal forms of stranger violence is to be devised, it appears that it will have to be done by circumventing measures of nonstranger violence. The major problem is that the victim does not, for reasons already discussed, feel inclined to either report these offenses on a victimization survey or report them to the police.

A final piece of evidence is available from the Gove, et al. (1985) comparison of the Uniform Crime Reporting Program and the NCS. Gove, et al. (1985) found eight studies that compared results from the NCS and the UCR. A study by Skogan (1974) was based on surveys in ten cities and reported correlations between the two data sources for only robbery and auto theft. For robbery, the NCS correlation with the Uniform Crime Reporting Program was .39; for auto theft, the correlation was .94. The results of the remaining seven studies, given in Table 3-2 are based on 26 cities and include the full sample of households and businesses.

It is known from city vicitimization surveys that the standard error is large because of sample size and interviewer effects. Further, many crimes reported on vicitimization survey are not reported to police, particluarly those involving nonstrangers, and the police often disagree with victims about how a crime should be classified. Given these difficulties, the correlations for auto theft, robbery and burglary in Table 3-2 are surprisingly large. The high correlations, ranging from .70 to .91, for motor vehicle theft are expected because insurance companies frequently require that the offenses be reported to the police.

Correlations for reports of robberies in the two data sources range from .62 to .81. The correlation for the Nelson study (Table 3-2) is for robbery with a weapon. In addition, Nelson adjusted the base population of data from the FBI (but not the victimization survey) to take into account the proportion of people commuting to the city on a daily basis.

For burglaries, the correlations in Table 3-2 range from .60 to .81. While the modification in the population base introduced by Nelson increased the robbery correlation, it depressed the correlation for burglaries.

The correlations for rape, ranging from .01 to .38, were among the smallest in Table 3-2. Gove et al. (1985) indicate that rapes reported in the Uniform Crime Reporting Program are more likely to be completed

Table 3-2

The NCS-UCR Correlations Reported in Seven
Studies of NCS Cities*

Decker et. al. (1982: 30)	Cohen and Lichback (1982: 262)[b]
r = .90 Motor Theft	r = .82 Motor Theft
.79 Robbery	.72 Robbery
.69 Burglary	.73 Burglary
.01 Rape	.10 Rape
-.39 Agg. Assault	-.39 Agg. Assault

Nelson (1979: 26)
   r =   .91 Motor Theft
      .81 Robbery with weap.
      .69 Burglary
      .56 Robb. without weap.
      .04 Rape
     -.36 Agg. Assault

Decker (1980: 53)
   r =   .86 Motor Theft
      .65 Robbery
      .81 Burglary
      .38 Rape
     -.12 Agg. Assault

Cohen and Land (1984)[a]
   r =   .82 Motor Theft
      .78 Robbery
      .74 Burglary
      .13 Rape
     -.36 Agg. Assault

Clarren and Schwartz (1976: 124)
   r =   .85 Motor Theft
      .66 Robbery
      .76 Burglary
      .06 Rape
     -.56 Agg. Assault

Booth et. al. (1977: 119)
   r =   .70 Auto Theft
      .62 Robbery
      .60 Burglary

[a]Correlation after natural log transformation.

[b]The surveys in the 13 cities which were surveyed twice were treated as independent; thus, n = 39.

*Taken from Gove, Hughes, and Geerken (1985: 478).

acts and more likely to meet legal criteria with respect to the use of force or threat of force. These ingredients are particularly difficult to establish if there is a prior relationship between offender and victim.

This is not to suggest, the authors add, that rapes reported in victimization surveys are trivial events. It is to suggest that while they may be highly traumatic events to the victim, rapes reported in victimization surveys are probably less serious in terms of physical violence and present more ambiguous evidence with respect to legal criteria.

Correlations between the two data sources for aggravated assault are uniformly negative, ranging from -.12 to -.56. Preceding sections have shown that while police statistics underreport the number of assaults in which the offender is known or related to the victim, the underreporting of victimization surveys is even more pronounced. The inverse correlations probably reflect the greater number of assaults involving acquaintances and relatives in data from the Uniform Crime Reporting Program in comparison with the NCS.

Gove et al. (1985) suggest that crimes tabulated by the police must service a filtering process consisting of citizen reporting and police definition. Crimes that result in injury to the victim, loss of property with considerable value, and those committed by strangers form most of the cases reported by the Uniform Crime Reporting program. Even for rapes and aggravated assaults, for which the correlation between the two data sources is weak, there is considerable evidence to suggest that the events reported to the police are the most serious:

> Official crime rates are in part a measure of the extent to which citizens feel injured, frightened, and financially hurt by a criminal act. In this sense they may be a better measure of social disruption than are "true rates," where more objectively defineable behavior is measured. In short, the rates of the index crimes presented in the UCR appear to be reasonably good approximations of true crime rates when the latter are defined as what both citizens and the police view as serious violations of the laws which codify the fundamental personal and property norms of society. (Gove, et al., 1985: 489,491)

If most nonstranger violence is not viewed as serious enough to report and if Gove and his colleagues are correct, then it is unlikely that any accurate measure of non-fatal violence involving nonstrangers will be forthcoming from official statistics.

REFERENCES

Beattie, R. H. (1962). Problems of criminal statistics in the United States. In M. E. Wolfgang, L. Savitz, and N. Johnston (Eds.), The sociology of crime and delinquency, (pp. 37-43). New York: John Wiley.

Berk, R., Loseke, D., Berk, S. F. & Rauma, D. (1980). Bringing the cops back in: A study of efforts to make the criminal justice system more responsive to incidents of family violence. Social Science Research, 9, 193-215.

Berk, R. & Loseke, D. (1981). Handling family violence: The situational determinants of police arrests in domestic disturbances. Law and Society Review, 15, 317-346.

Block, R. (1974). Why notify the police: The victim's decision to notify the police of an assault. Criminology, 11, 555-569.

Bureau of Justice Statistics (1982). Violent crime by strangers. Washington: U.S. Government Printing Office.

Bureau of Justice Statistics (1987). Violent Crime by Strangers and Nonstrangers. Washington: U.S. Government Printing Office.

Curtis, L. A. (1974). Criminal violence: National patterns and behavior. Lexington: Lexington Books.

Ennis, P. H. (1967a). Criminal victimization in the United States: A report of a national survey. Washington: U.S. Government Printing Office.

Ennis, P. H. (1967b). Crime, victims, and the police. Trans-Action, June, 36-44.

Gottfredson, M. R. & Gottfredson, D. M. (1988). Decision making in criminal justice: Toward the rational exercise of discretion. New York: Plenum Press.

Gove, W. R., Hughes, M. & Geerken, M. (1985). Are Uniform Crime Reports a valid indicator of index crimes? An affirmative answer with some minor qualifications. Criminology, 23, 451- 501.

Hindelang, M. J., Gottfredson, M. R. & Garofalo, J. (1978). Victims of personal crime: An empirical foundation for a theory of personal victimization. Cambridge: Ballinger.

Lehnen, R. G. & Skogan, W. G. (1981). The National Crime Survey: Working papers, Vol. 1: Current and Historical Perspectives, (NCJ-75374). Washington: U.S. Government Printing Office.

Lejeune, R. & Alex, N. (1973). On being mugged: The event and its aftermath. Urban Life and Culture, 2, 259-287.

Lejins, P. (1966). Uniform Crime Reports. University of Michigan Law Review, 64, 1011-1030.

Mendelsohn, B. (1963). The origin of the doctrine of victimology. Excerpta Criminologica, 3, 239-244.

Mulvihill. D. J., Tumin. M. M. & Curtis. L. A. (1969). Crimes of violence, (A Staff Report to the National Commission on the Causes and Prevention of Violence, Volume 11) Washington: U.S. Government Printing Office.

Petersen, W. (1975). Population. New York: Macmillan.

Robison, S. M. (1966). A critical review of the Uniform Crime Reports. University of Michigan Law Review, 64, 1031-1054.

Schneider, A. L. (1981). Differences between survey and police information about crime. In R. G. Lehnen and W. G. Skogan (Eds.), The National Crime Survey: Working Papers Vol. 1: Current and Historical Perspectives. (pp. 39-46). Washington: U.S. Government Printing Office.

Sellin, T. (1962). The significance of records of crime. In M. E. Wolfgang, L. Savitz, and N. Johnston (Eds.), The sociology of crime and delinquency (pp. 59-68). New York: John Wiley.

Skogan, W. G. (1976). Citizen reporting of crime: Some national panel data. Criminology, 13, 535-549.

Skogan. W. G. (1982). Issues in the measurement of victimization, (NCJ-74682). Washington: U.S. Government Printing Office.

Sparks. R. F. (1982). Research on victims of crime: Accomplishments, issues and new directions, (DHHS Publication No. (ADM) 82-1091). Washington: U.S. Government Printing Office.

Turner, A. G. (1981). The San Jose recall study. In R. G. Lehnen and W. G. Skogan (Eds), The National Crime Survey: Working Papers Vol 1: Current and Historical Perspectives. (pp. 22-27). Washington: U.S. Government Printing Office.

von Hentig, H. (1948). The criminal and his victim. New Haven: Yale University Press.

Wolfgang, M. E. (1963). Uniform Crime Reports: A critical appraisal. University of Pennsylvania Law Review, 111, 708-738.

Wolfgang, M. E. (1958). Patterns in criminal homicide. Philadelphia: University of Pennsylvania Press.

Yngvesson, B. B. (1978). The Atlantic fisherman. In L. Nader and H. F. Todd, Jr. (Eds.), The disputing process--law in ten societies (pp. 239-252). New York: Columbia University Press.

Zimring, F. (1972). The medium is the message: Firearms caliber as a determinant of death from assault. <u>Journal of Legal Studies</u>, <u>1</u>, 97-123.

CHAPTER 4

WHO ARE STRANGERS?

In the preceding chapters on the statistics of stranger violence, an important preliminary question was deliberately overlooked: what is stranger violence? The difficulty with the question is not in deciding that intentional injury or death inflicted on another is violence, but in deciding what is meant by the relationship that is given the term of "stranger."

The present chapter is the first of several to consider theoretical issues related to an understanding of stranger violence. Its purpose is to examine and evaluate the various definitions and perspectives on stranger relationships that are relevant to an understanding of violence. Most of the sparse theoretical literature on stranger relationships is incomplete, inadequately conceptualized, and tangentially relevant to a formulation that can be applied to stranger violence. This and later chapters will provide, it is hoped, a more useful and coherent formulation.

It is important to furnish some theoretical criteria against which to evaluate the available definitions and perspectives. The first is a need for a positive definition of stranger relationships. Examination of the research literature on stranger violence shows that it typically is defined in relation to other kinds of victim/offender relationships, when it is defined at all. To argue that stranger homicides are those in which there is "no prior relationships" is to view the term in regard to relationships in which there is a prior relationship, such as a friend or family member. While this may be a useful methodological expedient, the lack of a positive definition has several consequences that make theoretical development of the area difficult, if not impossible.

A second point turns upon what is meant by the concept of "stranger." It is an oversimplification to say strangers are people who are unknown. Is an unknown Sydneysider in Australia a stranger in the same way as the unknown person who just walked into your office, or the people you see as you proceed down a busy city street? How about the black family who moved into the white neighborhood a year ago? Nobody seems to "know" them. Are its members strangers in the same sense as that person who entered your office?

Such questions highlight the different meanings of the term stranger and indicate conceptual clarification is essential to understanding stranger homicide and violence. From the time a person steps outside his or her home in a city until that person's return to private space, interaction with strangers is likely to occur in order to accomplish routine tasks. Out of the large number of stranger encounters, some very small fraction results in violence for a few people. For an even smaller subset, murder will occur. In other words, because violent and fatal encounters develop out of or are built upon social expectations involved in routine interaction, a notion of stranger relationships useful to explaining violence among strangers must be relevant to non-violent behavior as well.

The Need for a Positive Definition

Researchers who have used police files for homicide research have employed victim/offender categories as if the meaning of various relationship were self-evident. Others have indicated explicitly the source of their definitions; Munford, Kazer, Feldman, and Stivers (1976) state, "the victim was killed by <u>a relative or acquaintance or by a stranger</u> if the record so indicated" (italics in the original) (p. 215).

A few investigators have shown a concern for the theoretical problem by providing a negative definition. Wolfgang, for example, defined a stranger as "one with whom no known previous contact existed." (Wolfgang, 1958: 205).

Greater sensitivity to the theoretical aspects was shown by Wolfgang's effort to develop a theoretically relevant classification of victim/offender relationships. He divided criminal homicides into "primary" contacts (family members, close friends, paramours and homosexual partners) and "non-primary" contacts (acquaintances, strangers, sex rivals, enemies, felons or police officers, and innocent bystanders). Although Wolfgang did not develop the idea further, he suggested that a primary relationship generally was one in which there was a <u>Gemeinschaft</u> level of interaction. This type of interaction is characterized by (1) an unspecialized and general level of interaction, encompassing the whole person rather than limited spheres of his existence, (2) a small group, and (3) informal rather than highly controlled or predictable patterns of interaction (Boskoff, 1972). The use of the term non-primary rather than the term secondary seems to suggest a negative definition: what cannot be classified as primary becomes non-primary.

The above distinction between primary and non-primary homicides was used by Mulvihill and Tumin (1969) in a staff report for the National Commission on the Causes and Prevention of Violence. Curtis (1974) also employed the terms in reporting the results of a seventeen-city study and in his time series analysis of the Supplementary Homicide Reports for 1963-1972. For the latter, Curtis constructed a category of "non-primary relationship---mostly strangers" by combining the SHR categories of "known felony type" and "suspected felony type" as an approximate measure of stranger relationships.

Homicides were also classified as primary and non-primary in a study of the relationship between deterrence and homicide by Parker and Smith (1979). The authors asserted that one of the problems with previous research was that it treated homicide as a unidimensional phenomenon; its relationship to deterrence could be better understood, it was claimed, if homicide was divided into primary and non-primary types. Primary homicide "involves family or acquaintances and is usually an act of passion" (Parker and Smith, 1979: 615). Non-primary homicides were said to be "often instrumental in nature in that they generally occur in the commission of another crime" (Parker and Smith, 1979: 615).[1]

Using a multiple regression analysis, they regressed primary and non-primary homicide rates against variables measuring the severity and certainty of punishment. In addition, they included several etiological variables: a structural poverty index, percentage of the population in the southern region, percentage nonwhite, urban, and aged 20-34.

Parker and Smith (1979) concluded that a homicide model emphasizing etiological variables was better supported than one using structural variables (certainty and severity of punishment). Further, distinguishing between the two types of homicide was useful because the etiological variables associated with homicide were better predictors of primary homicides than non-primary ones.

Although used in several research studies, the distinction between primary and non-primary homicides has received little theoretical development. The distinction has been used most often as a device to classify data for further analysis. Beyond Wolfgang's reference to the Gemeinschaft quality of primary homicides, both concepts have been applied as if their meaning was self-evident.

Largely because non-primary homicides lack any clear theoretical referents, there is little consensus about the type of homicides that should be included in the category. For example, Wolfgang (1958) embraces secondary relationships (acquaintances, felon or police officer), stranger relationships, and conflict relationships (sex rival, enemy). On the other hand, Parker and Smith (1979) include gangland slayings, homicides occurring in criminal and mental institutions, felony homicides, and suspected felony homicides; the last mostly homicides involving strangers. In a somewhat different vein, Curtis (1974) uses non-primary to refer to felony homicides and suspected felony homicides. Rather than reflecting any theoretical concerns, the homicides classified as non-primary reflect the data available to the investigator. While Wolfgang used homicide data from police files, Parker and Smith, and Curtis used data from the SHR.

The existence of negative definitions of stranger relationships also characterizes victimization surveys. The Bureau of Justice Statistics reports (1982, 1987), discussed in the preceding chapter, define crimes by strangers as "those committed by total strangers, in which the assailant was completely unknown to the victim, and those in which the assailant was known only by sight" (1987: 1).

The theoretical difficulties associated with negative definitions are similar to the problems encountered with what Parsons has called "residual categories."

> Every system, including both its theoretical propositions and its main relevant empirical insights, may be visualized as an illuminated spot enveloped by darkness. The logical name for the darkness is, in general, "residual categories". . . . If, as is almost always the case, not all the actually observable facts of the field, or those which have been observed, fit into sharply, positively defined categories, they tend to be given one or more blanket names which refer to categories negatively defined, that is, of facts known to exist, which are even more or less adequately described, but which are defined theoretically by their failure to fit into the positively defined categories of the system. The only theoretically significant

statement that can be made about these facts are negative statements - they are <u>not</u> so and so. But it is not to be inferred that because these statements are negative they are therefore unimportant. (Parsons, 1968: 17-18)

It is not that defining stranger homicide and violence residually precludes empirical inquiry. Rather it is that when stranger violence is defined residually, it tends to be ignored or to be confounded with other variables when conceptualizing its role in empirical inquiry. Sampson has noted that on "the empirical side, previous examination of personal victimization has for the most part lumped together crimes by acquaintances and crimes by strangers, even though there is no <u>a priori</u> reason to expect that the patterns of stranger crime are necessarily the same as acquaintance crime" (Sampson, 1987: 328).

The matter can be illustrated by considering the "lifestyles" theory of personal criminal victimization developed by Hindelang, Gottfredson, and Garofalo (1978). Lifestyles, according to the authors, refer to routine activities---"a characteristic way of distributing one's time, one's interest, and one's talent among the common social roles of adult life" (Hindelang, et al., 1978: 245). The theory can be summarized as follows:

> In our model, lifestyle differences result from differences in role expectations, structural constraints, and individual and subcultural adaptations. Variations in lifestyles are related differentially to probabilities of being in particular places at particular times and coming into contact with persons who have particular characteristics; because criminal victimization is not randomly distributed across time and space and because offenders in personal crimes are not representative of the general population---but rather there are high risk times, places, and people---this implies that lifestyle differences are associated with differences in <u>exposure</u> to situations that have a high victimization risk. (Italics in the original) (Hindelang, et al., 1978: 245)

In relation to stranger violence, the fourth proposition of the theory suggests that an "individual's chances of personal victimization are dependent upon the extent to which the individual shares demographic characteristics with offenders" (Hindelang, et al., 1978: 257). While the proposition holds for many types of personal violence, it does not hold for race in regard to robbery victims and offender when the offender is a stranger. According to a Bureau of Justice Statistics report (1982), 51 percent of the robbery victimization among strangers involves white victims and black offenders. In other words, a proposition of demographic similarity between victim and offender serves to obscure an important characteristic of stranger violence, given the controversial nature of interracial crime. The proposition also ignores the finding in the Memphis research and in the eight city study that stranger homicides involve young offenders and older victims (Riedel, 1981; Riedel and Zahn, 1985).

The lack of "sharp, positively defined categories" of victim/offender relationships also leads to some confusion in a discussion of proposition six of the lifestyles theory. It asserts that the "probability of personal victimization, particularly personal theft, increases as a function of the proportion of time that an individual spends among nonfamily members" (Hindelang, et al., 1978: 260). While the authors discuss the research related to stranger victimization, "nonfamily" relationships are not limited to strangers. The broad category of friends and acquaintances and its relationship to personal victimization are treated as if they are identical to stranger relationships.

Sampson (1987) takes a similar position in his discussion of lifestyle and routine activities theory:

> Most importantly, there are strong theoretical reasons for distinguishing stranger victimizations that derive from the lifestyle-routine activity and opportunity theories originated by Hindelang and colleagues (1978) and by Cohen and Felson (1979, 1980, 1981). The explanatory constructs developed, such as routine daily activities, guardianship, target attractiveness, and lifestyle, lead to crucial hypotheses regarding victimization by strangers. For example, the theories predict that an increase in routine activities away from the household increases contact with strangers, thereby decreasing guardianship and increasing stranger victimization risk. On the other hand, family violence and conflict with friends and acquaintances may be simultaneously decreased. Unfortunately, empirical tests of routine activity theory have, to date, used crime rates and victimization rates that aggregate and confound primary and stranger crimes, precluding further refinement of the opportunity model. (Sampson, 1987: 328-329)

The major casualties in residual definitions are conceptual and theoretical. The idea of stranger violence is ignored or is combined with other categories, such as violence involving acquaintances, in the conceptualization of empirical inquiry. Generalizations that are made about the combined categories may characterize violence involving acquaintances better than violence involving strangers. Not only is knowledge about stranger violence not available, but a significant opportunity to refine existing theory is lost.

The major problem is that it is difficult, if not impossible, to theorize about a negative state. To state relationships about a phenomenon means that it must be defined in terms of positive characteristics. Though criminological classifications have relied on residual definitions, sociologists have developed positive and general theoretical approaches to the study of stranger relationships. This will become evident in the following discussion of Simmel's (1964) essay on the stranger, Robert Park (1928) and Everett Stonequist's (1937) writings on the marginal man, and Mary Margaret Wood's (1934) conception of the stranger as "newcomer." The question is how these approaches contribute directly or indirectly to an understanding of stranger violence.

PERSPECTIVES ON STRANGER RELATIONSHIPS

Simmel and Strangers

Discussion of the relationship of a stranger to a group must begin with Simmel's (1964) short essay on the subject. Donald Levine and his colleagues describe the essay as the segment of Simmel's work that had the earliest and perhaps the most important impact on American sociological research (Levine, Carter, and Gorman, 1976a). Written in 1908, Der Fremde (The Stranger) forms part of a larger chapter in Simmel's Soziologie, a book that discusses the relationship between physical space and social interaction. "The Stranger" was first translated by Robert Park for inclusion in the classic textbook, Introduction to the Science of Sociology (Park and Burgess, 1924).[2]

The need for a positive definition of stranger relationships was clear to Simmel: "to be a stranger is naturally a very positive relation: it is a specific form of interaction." What distinguishes the unknown person from the stranger is the possibility of interaction. The nature of this limited exclusion is evident in Simmel's observation that the "inhabitants of Sirius are not really strangers to us, at least not in any sociologically relevant sense: they do not exist at all" (Simmel, 1964:402).[3] In the essay introducing Simmel's writings, Levine (1971) suggests that four basic presuppositions underlie Simmel's analyses: form, reciprocity, distance, and dualism. While all four are present in the essay on the stranger, three of them, form, distance, and dualism, are particularly useful in understanding Simmel's insights.

Simmel, it will be remembered, refers to the stranger in terms of a "specific form of interaction." (Emphasis added) Form and content are major analytical concepts for Simmel; the difficulty is that their meanings tend to shift with different contexts, what is content in one aspect of social life becomes form in another (Weingartner, 1959).

To think, Simmel suggests, is to divide the world into form and content. Forms are a way of organizing the vast variety of objects of art and artifact, theories and religious dogmas, philosophical systems, social institutions, and conventions of behavior to provide meaning, structure and stability. The task of sociology is to create forms of sociation or interaction that underlie the varieties of content.

Forms are not, however, general ideas developed by generalization and abstraction. The emphasis is not on their abstract nature, but on the process of abstracting them. Forms derive their direction and thrust from historical knowledge and perspective.

> Abstraction for Simmel is not---it could not be---abstraction from content---phenomena in which the forms inhere and through which alone they can be set forth, but abstraction from content---perspective. Abstracting must be understood in the radical sense of extracting or extricating from reality something which is not a directly observable and common element in it. (Tenbruck, 1965: 78-79)

Forms are cultural creations, but they have the interesting characteristic that as they grow and develop, they appear to take on a life of their own. When they become highly developed, they turn on their creator and confront him or her: they make demands. For example, exchange began between people as a simple way of obtaining from others something that they had and did not need. It represents a social form created to further practical activities. As they become highly developed, economic systems impose demands on the people involved in them, often in ways that cannot be understood or controlled. We need only look at the problem of unemployment and inflation in recent economic history to recognize the presence of a form that often confronts its creator in incomprehensible and unpleasant ways.

The analytical usefulness of social forms stems from the fact that, while they are relatively persistent, a given form embraces apparently quite diverse content. There are, for example, similarities in behavior in the court of a king and in the main offices of a corporation, both of which can be subsumed under the social forms of superordination and subordination (Coser, 1965).

With respect to the stranger, the social form specifies a determinate relationship to the group:

> He is fixed within a particular spatial group, or with a group whose boundaries are similar to spatial boundaries. But his position in this group is determined, essentially, by the fact that he has not belonged to it from the beginning, that he imports qualities into it, which do not and cannot stem from the group itself. (Simmel, 1964: 40)

Simmel's description of a stranger being in the group, but not of it[4] refers to the location of the stranger form. Yet there are a variety of contents that can be included under this form. Simmel discussed the role of the trader in economic history while Coser (1965) concluded that Simmel's inability to reach the higher academic ranks until shortly before his death was a consequence of his role as a stranger in the academic establishment.

Forms are given unity and inner articulation through their dualistic nature. Dualism is the view that the "world can best be understood in terms of conflicts and contrasts between opposed categories" (Levine, 1971: xxxv). Dualism is used in different ways in Simmel's theory. Sometimes opposed qualities are seen as developing from an undifferentiated unity, sometimes they are seen as a synthesis of love and hate (Levine, 1971).

Concerning the social form of the stranger, dualism appears as a midpoint between opposing categories of distance, a unity that cannot be expressed directly. Thus, if wandering and establishment at a fixed point are conceptual opposites, then "the sociological form of 'stranger' presents the unity, as it were, of these two characteristics" (Simmel, 1964: 402).

Distance has been mentioned with respect to a particular kind of dualism, but distance has a general role to play in Simmel's theory. Forms are given properties and meanings as a function of distance between people or between people and objects (Levine, 1971). In appearing to acquire a life of their own as they grow, they develop away from the subject; there is a distance created between the subject and object, which gives the social form its meaning and characteristics. Subject areas like Art, Music, and Economics represent forms that have developed to a point where there is a large distance between subject and object. Among individuals, social forms such as secrecy may serve to increase the distance between people. On the other hand, conflict brings distant people together (Simmel, 1964).

The stranger is defined as a unique combination of opposing categories of distance.

> The unity of nearness and remoteness involved in every human relation is organized, in the phenomenon of the stranger, in a way which may be more briefly formulated by saying that in the relationship to him, distance means that he, who is close by, is far, and strangeness means that he, who also is far, is actually near. (Simmel, 1964: 402)

The formal nature of the stranger, therefore, refers to a determinate relationship to a group that cannot be specified directly, but whose meaning and properties can be expressed as a unique combination of nearness and farness.

Simmel illustrates the social form of the stranger by looking at one particular content, the trader. Traders are found throughout economic history, but they are strangers everywhere outside their home or town. Traders are needed for purposes of exchange, but they are never members of the host group. Traders are not accepted because, by nature, they have no position that gives them permanence. They are no "'owner of soil' - soil not only in the physical, but also in the figurative sense of a life-substance which is fixed" (Simmel, 1964: 403). The relation of the trader to the group is, of course, reciprocal, but the position of the trader imports certain characteristics to the reciprocity. These characteristics formally reflect the "unity of nearness and remoteness" that defines the stranger.

Simmel uses social distance in at least three different senses. First, he refers to distance in terms of ecological attachment and mobility. The stranger is not bound to any particular group by kinship, locality or occupation; he or she can come into contact with every group and group member. This "specific characteristic" of mobility "embodies that synthesis of nearness and distance which constitutes the formal position of the stranger" (Simmel, 1964: 403-404).

Second, because the stranger is not committed to any particular group, he or she acquires an attitude of objectivity. In Simmel's view, objectivity is not passivity and detachment, but "a particular structure of distance and nearness, indifference and involvement." (Simmel, 1964: 404)

The objectivity of the stranger means that he or she is not bound by commitments that would prejudice his or her judgment. Such presumed objectivity appears in the practice of some Italian cities who called in judges from the outside to settle cases. The native inhabitants were presumed to lack objectivity because of entanglements in family and party interests. In contemporary times, attempts to avoid local prejudgments are reflected in the efforts of lawyers to obtain a change of venue in criminal cases.

Because objectivity involves a specific kind of participation, a structure of "indifference and involvement," the stranger may be the recipient of confidences that would be withheld from a closely related person. The position of the stranger as trusted confidant is often played out in the traditional role of therapist. Information which a patient cannot discuss with family or close friends may be freely shared with a therapist because of presumed objectivity and distance from the patient's family and friends. The specific kind of participation suggested here represents, of course, cultivated skills reinforced by a fee for service.

In a society like ours that is so zealously committed to openness and candor in human relationships, it is difficult to ascertain just how applicable Simmel's insights on the stranger as confidant are. While everyone certainly applauds the concern for honesty in human relationships, all too often it turns into a kind of "psychological exhibitionism," a need to tell anyone who will listen the most intimate details of one's life. On some occasions, a person wishes that openness and candor were tempered with the interdicts of good taste.

From another point of view, the freedom associated with objectivity has dangerous possibilities. In a conflict, the attacked party may attribute difficulties to the provocation of strangers. Such was the case in the sixties when, in the view of the inhabitants of small southern towns, disorder and conflicts over civil rights were the "work of outside agitators."

Finally, in what is probably the most frequent understanding of the term, social distance may refer to the extent to which common features help to identify the individual as a group member or as a stranger.

> For, the common features are basically determined in their effect upon the relation by the question whether they exist only between the participants in this particular relationship, and thus are quite general in regard to this relation, but are specific and incomparable in regard to everything outside of it---or whether the participants feel that these features are common to them because they are

common to a group, a type, or mankind in general.   (Simmel,
1964: 405)

Where the features are common to a group or a type, it causes a
quality of abstractness that is a characteristic of stranger relationships.
Because the stranger has only the more general features in common with
the group, the relationship is of a more abstract nature.   By contrast,
because group members know one another in terms of specific
differences, they are "organically" connected.

This particular view of social distance can be made clearer by
considering its pervasiveness in another apparently unrelated instance.
Simmel suggests that a "trace of strangeness . . . enters even the most
intimate relationship."   In the first blush of romantic attachment, the
lovers feel that there has never been a love like theirs; their feelings for
the other person are unique and incomparable.   "He or she is not like the
others, he or she is different" is a common sentiment.   Estrangement
begins when the feeling of uniqueness vanishes, and when the relationship
is seen to have "no inner and exclusive necessity."   The lovers come to
recognize that in their relationship they carry out:

only a generally human destiny; that they experience an experience
that has occurred a thousand times before; that, had they not
accidentally met their particular partner, they would have found the
same significance in another person. (Simmel, 1964: 406)

It is difficult to point to any part of Simmel's essay as a <u>direct</u>
contribution to understanding stranger violence.   Given his dialectic
proclivity for providing surprising and unexpected insights into ideas
usually thought of in a conventional and mundane way, Simmel's
strangers were not the negative and fear provoking characters usually
associated with the category.   Quite the contrary, Simmel portrayed
strangers as having much freedom and success.   To be sure, the freedom
was structurally dependent on the development of money economy
(Simmel, 1978).   Thus, it is no accident that the stranger described in
most detail was one whose position was important to a money economy -
the trader (Levine, 1977).

Simmel's impact on theory about stranger behavior was indirect
rather than direct.   Virtually every theorist who has written on the topic
since Simmel has implicitly or explicitly relied on his formulation.
Consider, for example, the definition of stranger relationships. Based on
Simmel's view that the stranger is known only in terms of the general and
abstract characteristics of the group, Shaler (1904), Wood (1934), and
Lofland (1973) have indicated that strangers, in contrast to nonstrangers,

are known "categorically." In other words, it is not true that nothing is known about strangers: in an encounter with strangers, an identity is imputed to them based on general and abstract social categories. The stranger encountered can be characterized by racial and gender categories, the perceived age, height, and so forth. While such information may be minimal, it serves to determine expectations and guide interaction.

To categorize persons is the first step in devising rules about appropriate behavior. Such appropriate behavior may be spatial; categoric information, as Lofland (1973) has noted, can be linked to ecological settings. While spatial location helps to impute an identity, it is equally apparent that categoric and ecological information can be used to prevent encounters with undesirable strangers. For example, a publication of the National Safety Council (1974) designed to provide information on safety on the streets advises the following:

1. Avoid walking the street late at night.
2. Avoid narrow walkways between buildings at all times.
3. Walk with another person if possible.
4. Never take a short cut through poorly lighted areas.
5. Leave car in a well-lighted area when parking on the street at night.

The consonance between cognitive categories and ecological settings is consistent with Simmelian theory, but Simmel's view of the stranger suggests that following the rules of safety is no long-term guarantee. Another view of the objectivity, or freedom from group prejudice, that characterizes Simmel's stranger is one that suggests the stranger is capable of innovative approaches to social arrangements. Thus, what is viewed as prudent preventive strategies to a potential crime victim may be seen as tactical challenges to a violent stranger offender. The ecological precautions taken to prevent stranger assaults are seen as temporary obstacles to the offender.

The voiding of such precautions by violent victimization leads to more elaborate ecological and technological preventives that are again overcome by the offender. This escalating cat-and-mouse game ultimately has negative consequences for the victim. What was prudent crime prevention behavior for the urban dweller becomes a matter in which the fear of criminal victimization increasingly affects the quality of individual existence. In other words, do "target-hardening" technologies increasingly lock the offender out or the victim in?

Of course, Simmel's influence on later writers is not limited to a definition of stranger relationships as later sections will make clear

(McLemore, 1970; Levine, et al., 1976a, 1976b; Levine, 1977; Meyer, 1928). Indeed, so pervasive has been his influence that writers tend to confuse the origins of the different concepts of the stranger. Contemporary commentators, especially, tend to attribute to Simmel ideas about the stranger which more appropriately belong to Park, Stonequist, or Wood. Frequent citations to Simmel's essay "tend to be literary embellishments, a kind of respectful acknowledgment of Simmel's contribution" (McLemore, 1970:93). Many attributions, McLemore notes, might be made more appropriately to an intervening source.

To the extent that McLemore's conclusions are correct, Simmel underestimated the impact of his writings, although he clearly understood their ultimate consequences. In a passage written in his diary shortly before his death, he states:

> I know that I shall die without intellectual heirs, and that is as it should be. My legacy will be like cash, distributed to many heirs, each transforming his part into use according to <u>his</u> nature----a use which will no longer reveal its indebtedness to this heritage. (Quoted in Levine, 1971: xiii)

THE STRANGER AS MARGINAL MAN

The concept of the marginal man was first presented by Robert Park (1928) in an article on the consequences of migration. Social change occurs, Park suggested, not as a result of change in racial types of climate, but as the result of migration. Migration, with its attendant conflicts and fusions of people, is one of the decisive forces in history.

Contemporary forms of migration, like those which occurred in the United States, are different from earlier forms. Because of the ease and security of travel, and the development of national and international forms of communication, commerce, and industry, migration is no longer a matter of whole tribes or a larger social unit moving from one country to another. Modern migrations are generally private concerns, the migrants being led by the most varied of motives. Modern migration is a spasmodic movement of individuals rather than an organized movement of peoples.

Migration results in the release of the individual from social restraints and constraints. The release occurs because the individual to some extent has left behind the bindings of his or her old culture. It also occurs because the appearance of migrants in large numbers has a disruptive effect on the culture that receives them. Such cultural change and release leads to the emergence of a person who "learns to look upon the world in which he was born and bred with something of the detachment of the stranger" (Park, 1928: 888).

The process of assimilation does not proceed evenly in all cases. Where the migrant is characterized by distinctive and divergent physical characteristics, such as with Asians or blacks in the United States, there can be substantial obstacles to assimilation. Where such obstacles are absent and migrants are permitted to participate in the broader cultural life, as ultimately occurred with Jews, a new type personality appears. The new personality type is a "cultural hybrid," a person who could not break with his or her own past and traditions, yet was not quite accepted in the new society because of prejudice.

The marginal man is a person on the margin of two cultures and two societies that never completely interpenetrated and fused.

> The emancipated Jew was, and is, historically and typically the marginal man, the first cosmopolite and citizen of the world. He is par excellence the "stranger," who Simmel, himself a Jew, has described with such profound insight and understanding in his Soziologie. (Park, 1928: 892)

While the marginal man had the idealism, detachment, and sophistication of Simmel's cosmopolite, he was a person at odds with himself. The conflict of cultures expressed itself as divided self---the old self and the new. As a result, the marginal man was characterized by "spiritual instability, intensified self consciousness, restlessness, and malaise" (Park, 1928: 893). For many immigrants, "spiritual distress" was temporary, the result of a transitional state. For the marginal man, the crisis was apt to be more lasting.

Park's student, Everett Stonequist, substantially explicated and elaborated on the concept of marginal man. Stonequist (1937) began by observing that it is culture conflict that produces the marginal man.

> It is the conflict of groups possessing different cultures that is the determining influence in creating the marginal man, and the typical traits are social, psychological, rather than cultural, in nature. (Stonequist, 1937: 214)

Culture conflict is expressed through various processes of which migration is only one:

> The individual who through migration, education, marriage, or some other influence leaves one social group or culture without

adjusting to another finds himself on the margin of each, but a member of neither. He is a "marginal man." (Stonequist, 1937: 3)

While Stonequist broadened the idea of marginality substantially beyond Park's view, he spent very little time discussing instances of marginality that did not involve race or nationality. He does briefly take up the conflicts of the parvenu, the person who passes upward from one class status to another, the declasse, who has lost his class status, and the deracine, the country to city migrant. On a quite contemporary note, Stonequist discusses the marginality that will result from the transformation of women's roles.

The obvious type of marginal man is the person of mixed racial ancestry. This includes the mulattoes of the United States, the colored people of Jamaica, Hawaiians, and some inhabitants of Brazil. Such "racial hybrids," as a result of culture contacts, are often "cultural hybrids" as well. The relationship between racial and cultural hybrids is, however, one of overlap rather than identity. People may have a mixed culture without being of mixed race when the whole cultural system moves through cultural diffusion. The classic example, discussed at some length by Stonequist, has been the Jews.

To become a marginal man, the cultural or group conflict must be experienced as a personal problem. The "crisis experience" makes persons of certain racial or nationality groups aware that they are different, that they do not belong to the dominant cultural group. It is at this point that the characteristic traits of the marginal personality first appear. Minimally, the change in personality may involve a subtle sense of estrangement, malaise, and isolation. At the extreme, the conflicts may demoralize the individual, throwing him or her into such a state of disorganization that homicide, suicide, or psychosis may result.

The crisis experience and its resolution has been the theme of many works of fiction. In the novel A World Full of Strangers, for instance, Cynthia Freeman (1975) details the violent response of one of her main characters, David Rezinetsky, to a defining encounter with anti-Semitism. Rezinetsky is a successful insurance salesman in a predominantly Jewish section of New York. One day he is sent to meet his first gentile client in New Jersey. After waiting fruitlessly for almost four hours on a very hot day, he leaves the office, only to forget the handkerchief he had been using to mop his brow; when he returns, he overhears a conversation between the bookkeeper and his client's secretary.

"Well, you've got to give those Jew bastards a little credit. They've got plenty of moxie, they don't just give up. He could have sat here til hell froze over if you didn't get rid of him." The secretary laughed as the typewriter carriage came to an end and the bell rang.

"Over my dead body," she said.

The bookkeeper went on, "Those kikes ought to be locked up in a cage."

Someone had hit David between the eyes with a hammer. He jumped over the low railing, grabbed the bookkeeper by his tie, choking him, lifting off the stool and hitting him so hard he swayed back and forth like an automaton, then fell to the floor in a heap. David stood over the man; his face was swollen and blue, red blood seeping out of his mouth. Teeth clenched, David shouted, "This is one Jew bastard you're not going to forget in a hurry, you son-of-a-bitch." (Freeman, 1975: 71)

There are three typical modes of adjustment for persons caught in the clash of cultures. The first is the "nationalist role" in which the marginal man identifies with the subordinate or oppressed group. This type of adjustment is illustrated by Marcus Garvey's "Back to Africa" movement, Zionism, and various types of European nationalism.

Second, the marginal person may be assimilated into the dominant culture. Assimilation may require two generations or it may take the form of "passing" as a member of the dominant group where assimilation is not possible. This was the fate of David Rezinetsky in Freeman's novel. After the depicted violent episode, he changed his name to David Reed, moved to Chicago, and became highly successful in the insurance business. However, neither his son nor his wife were able to accept his choices and he eventually lost both of them.

The third type of adjustment involves the "intermediary role." Under some conditions, minority groups in a culture cannot demand self-government, but can claim political equality and the right to be religiously and culturally tolerated. "In such situations the marginal man is more likely to evolve into some intermediary role which leads to an accommodation and reapproachment between the clashing cultures: he often became an interpreter, conciliator, reformer, teacher" (Stonequist, 1937: 177).

It is important to pause here and consider the relationships among the writing of Stonequist, Park, and Simmel. In initially defining the marginal man, Park (1928) narrowly located the cause of marginality in the conditions of migration. The social psychological consequence of the immigrant who was not completely assimilated by one culture was the marginal man, "par excellence," the emancipated Jew.

For Stonequist, the generic cause of marginality was culture conflict, which could be expressed by migration, education, marriage, or a wide variety of other influences in which the person "leaves one social group or culture without making a satisfactory adjustment to another and finds himself on the margin of each, but a member of neither" (Stonequist, 1937: 3).

A broadening of causes corresponds to a broadening of effects. The emancipated Jew who was the major type of marginal man for Park became, for Stonequist, one representation of adjustment to cultural conflicts that generated marginality. The emancipated Jew was the typical marginal man for Park, but simply a special case of intermediary adjustment for Stonequist.

It is in their discussions of Jews as an example of the intermediary role that Stonequist and Park are most similar to Simmel. Stonequist describes the intermediary using Simmel's analysis of the stranger and his characteristics of objectivity, freedom from local prejudices, and mobility. Stonequist is clear that while the marginal man and the stranger may arise from the same conditions, the resulting mode of adjustment is quite distinct. The stranger is one who is not intimately or personally concerned with social activities around him.

> His relative detachment frees him from the self-consciousness, the divided loyalties of the marginal man. When the stranger seeks to identify himself integrally with the group in which he has moved, but is held at arm's length, he has evolved into the marginal position. (Stonequist, 1937: 178)

In other words, unlike the marginal man, Simmel's stranger does not aspire to be a member of a host group. Further, Stonequist suggests, Simmel's stranger maintains an instrumental relationship with the host group--that of a trader--while the marginal man has broad cultural relationships with two cultures. The latter qualifies the marginal man to play a uniquely creative role in mediating between the two cultures. The stranger may well emerge out of the same clash of cultures as the marginal man, but it is his unsuccessful adoption of a host group that turns him into the marginal man.

Other writers have used the concept of marginal man in one form or another to explain deviant behavior, crime and delinquency. The basic perspective of marginality locates pressure toward various forms of deviation or self-motivation toward deviation in persons who exist at the borders of two or more, usually incompatible, sets of values (Boskoff, 1972). Park and his colleagues sought to explain crime and delinquency in the "zone of transition" in cities where there were diverse cultures and racial categories. Besides Park, Burgess and McKenzie (1925), there was Thrasher's (1927) study in which juvenile gangs developed from casual street groups to unified and aggressive gangs. Thrasher found that gangs gave participants affection, respect, and recognition that was lacking, particularly when the parents were not assimilated into American culture. Other studies using the idea of marginality to explain crime or social problems included Young's (1932) work on Russian immigrants, Zorbaugh's (1929) study of the gold coast and the slum in Chicago, and Anderson's (1923) research on hobos.

More recent research has used the concept of marginality to explore conflicts unrelated to racial or ethnic differences. For example, Githens and Prestage (1978) examined the behavior and activity of women state legislators using Turner's (1964) analysis of marginality. Turner describes the marginal person as one who seeks to change his or her identification when he or she moves from one stratum to another, but is unable to do so because of incompatible value systems and organized group ties. For women legislators, their decision to seek political office also can mean the rejection of the values and norms of most other women. At the same time, the political groups with which the female legislator wishes to affiliate are reluctant to accept her.

In their study of 722 women state legislators, Githens and Prestage found some support for objective marginality. Women were well represented on committees, except for the important fiscal committees. But they tended to be assigned to committees that dealt with stereotypic female concerns such as health, welfare, and education. Women state legislators were also underrepresented in positions of leadership.

The women state legislators also experienced conflicting demands---experiential marginality. On the one hand, they reported a high level of self-motivation while, on the other, they attached great importance to family values. The subjects in the study did not report strong conflicts in regard to their feelings of success and influence.

It is difficult, however, to see the value of marginality in explaining violent crime between strangers. The cultural conflict that produces the marginal personality type may involve, as Stonequist (1937) suggests, such severe mental conflict that violent crime is an outcome. Such an extreme reaction would seem to require a more detailed theoretical specification than it receives by either Stonequist or Park. In short, the conceptual gap between the characteristics of women state legislators and those of a stranger homicide offender seem to be too great to be bridged by a single idea.

Second, marginality ignores the interaction between victim and offender in a violent encounter. As will be seen in future chapters, whether violence occurs between strangers is determined by the type of people that are in a setting, the nature of the setting, and the behavior of the victim. Assigning etiological significance to the marginal personality of the offender addresses only one of the dimensions that exist in such encounters.

Finally, the divided loyalties of the marginal man imply an attachment to the values of the victim and his group. The divided loyalties may be severe enough to cause the person to commit violence. But given his attachment to the victim's values, the violence is more likely to be directed to business associates, employers, and other acquaintances rather than strangers. In other words, marginality seems to contribute little to understanding the short and violent encounters that characterize anonymous victims and offenders in a contemporary urban setting.

THE STRANGER AS NEWCOMER

Park and Stonequist viewed the marginal man as the person caught between two cultures and suffering the psychological and social consequences of such a situation. The idea of the stranger can focus also on how an unknown person---the newcomer ---is accepted by the group. The most extensive theoretical development of this idea of the stranger was done by Wood (1934). Wood's analysis, although very good, has not stimulated the interest and research that followed Park and Stonequist's writings on marginal man. Wood (1934: 43) defines the stranger "as one who has come into face-to-face contact with the group for the first time." The requirement of "contact with the group" is the major focus of her explanation. However, whether a relationship with the stranger will develop, its possible duration and nature is "closely correlated with social relationships that are already present in the group which the stranger has entered" (Wood, 1934: 7). The importance of group structure and values are stated in her concluding chapter.

The broad determinant throughout is the character of the values about which the group is organized and the degree to which the stranger is adjudged an asset or a liability for the realization of such values, whether they pertain to kinship or to nationality, to expediency or to congeniality. (Wood, 1934: 284)

Even in the most ill-assorted aggregation of strangers, social relationships and "group forming" features are present. Rush hour in the New York subways may appear to be devoid of social relationships and lacking all cohesion. But even under those circumstances, there is:

relationship, mutual understanding, and agreement of a very definite character . . . the need of the elderly and the weak may be overlooked, and generally it is; but if it is actually observed, a seat or other assistance will be offered. (Wood, 1934: 49)

The first response of group members upon meeting a stranger is the social-psychological one of categorizing him or her. The tendency to form categories and evaluate people on that basis is what Wood, borrowing from Shaler (1904), calls the "categoric motive." Such categorizing is, however, limited and susceptible to stereotyping. If the stranger belongs to a different race toward which the group has a pre-existing negative attitude, he or she may be stereotyped by racial epithets and prevented from joining the group.

The concept of categoric motive receives more extensive development in Lofland's (1973) theory. For her, categorical knowledge of the stranger is an essential part of the definition of stranger relationships and the interaction between strangers. Wood, however, goes in another direction. She is interested in how and what is done with this categoric knowledge by a social group.

The treatment of the stranger, Wood believes, is determined by three overlapping and interacting sets of factors:

1. The nature of the fundamental system of social integration found in primitive societies and nations.
2. Local patterns of social integration that develop within the larger configuration and the bearing these relationships have on how the stranger is received.
3. In addition, there are a variety of circumstances that affect a particular contact. In other words, a particular contact between stranger and group is the outcome, in part, of a unique combination of variables.

How the stranger is treated is determined at the most general level by the system of social integration. In primitive societies, such as that of the Australian aborigines, a person's position was defined by an extensive system of kinship. Before a stranger could be admitted to the group, it was necessary to determine his or her relationship to every person in the group so that the proper term of address could be used. Where the relationship could not be assigned, the stranger was killed (Wood, 1934).

In contemporary societies, the concepts of citizenship and nationality provide the basis for integration and the dimensions that influence how the newcomer will be received. Nationality exists where social consciousness is diffused through the various classes: such consciousness provides a basis for racial and economic equality. Within this context, a stranger of a different race may be accepted legally, but not socially.

Local patterns develop within this large configuration, however, and group relationships have a bearing on how the stranger is received. Wood examines several instances of local configurations: immigrant communities, foreign colonies, frontier settlements, backward districts, rural neighborhoods, small towns, and cities. Immigrant communities will be considered as illustrative.

While other writers have been concerned with how the immigrant adapted to the dominant culture, this is not a central problem for Wood. For her, the major issue revolves around the newcomers or stranger-immigrants <u>vis-a-vis</u> the immigrant community. The problem of strangers is as "marginal man," but with respect to a semi-assimilated community of new immigrants. Thus, the first Jewish immigrants to the United States were Sephardic Jews, followed by German Jews, and finally, Polish and Russian Jews. As later groups poured in, the Sephardic Jews, who stood on the brink of assimilation, were often resentful and angry because succeeding groups threatened their hard-won status in the community.

Much the same happened with blacks in northern cities. The northern black inhabitants had grown accustomed to a large measure of freedom and equality. With the arrival of black migrants from the South during World War I, the resident blacks found themselves the object of dislike, prejudice, and discrimination for which they held the migrants responsible.

Not all instances are as clear cut as the preceding, because immigrant communities are themselves caught in the thros of change. The old social order in immigrant communities is disintegrating more rapidly than an alternative organization can be created. Thus, Wood concludes that behavior toward the stranger vacillates "now in this direction and now in that."

While the social structure of the group in relation to the newcomer is important, the exact contour of any given relationship is dependent upon events in the specific situation. One of the most important situational factors is the degree of mobility of the stranger. Degree of mobility for Wood refers to the amount of time or duration of contact with the group. This means that some relationships with strangers may be more or less temporary, but are, nonetheless, a matter of moment in determining the relationship of the stranger to the group.

Earlier, it was noted that characteristics of the stranger discussed by Simmel, such as mobility and objectivity, were based on social distance. No one characteristic had a higher logical priority than another. Wood, by contrast, uses degree of mobility as the concept out of which other characteristics flow. Of the characteristics listed by Simmel:

> mobility would seem to belong to a somewhat different and more general order than the rest, inasmuch as the degree of mobility which is present determines to a considerable extent the existence of all the other attributes. They are derived from it. (Wood, 1934: 247)

In other words, the degree of mobility leads to a more or less temporary relationship to the group. This condition will, in turn, result in the Simmelian characteristics of the stranger: objectivity, trusted confidant, and abstract relations.

It is worth pausing here to admire Wood's adroit assimilation of Simmelian theory. First, degree of mobility is assigned a higher priority than the other characteristics of the stranger enumerated by Simmel. Second, in interpreting degree of mobility of the stranger in terms of duration of contacts, she is viewing the stranger from the perspective of the group rather than the perspective of the stranger. Because a stranger may have contacts with many groups, the duration of contacts with a given group must necessarily be short; therefore, the relationship is temporary.

What are the consequences of these interpretative assumptions? If the relationship of the Simmelian stranger to the group is temporary, then his or her existence cannot have the generality of group-related factors that persist in time. The net effect of Wood's analysis is to reduce the explanatory importance of Simmelian concepts. The Simmelian stranger may be important in some settings to explain the "exact contour" of events in a specific situation, but his or her appearance is secondary in importance to the operation of group related factors.

The latter can be illustrated further by examining the two theorists' differing views of the permanence of the stranger's status. Wood focused on the newcomer as a stranger in the process of being accepted or rejected by the group. With that emphasis, how can the status of the stranger be permanent, as suggested by Simmel? Wood's response is to suggest that the stranger's status is permanent relative to groups in general, but not a given group. In the case of a given group it is temporary and, therefore, the factors that account for it are of secondary importance.

On the face of it, Wood's analysis would seem to have something important to contribute to an understanding of violent and non-violent encounters among strangers. The focus of the inquiry is on the initial contacts between strangers. There are, however, several problems that limit its application to the problem of stranger violence.

First, there is the persistent emphasis on the relationship of the stranger to other strangers as members of some group. Focus on the relationship of stranger to the group assumes that the group existed before the stranger. The stranger, so to speak, arrived after the rules of the interactional game had been established and the players chosen. Whether the stranger would be allowed to play in this game, whether he or she wanted to play, and what role, if any, he or she would play constituted the focus of theoretical explanation.

What is essential to remember in this analogy is that the group-individual relationship discussed refers to a group that receives support and is integrated with the broader culture and society. Lacking that legitimization, it might be possible to suggest that Wood's analysis would be appropriate for encounters between a single victim and a group of delinquent-stranger offenders. However, such delinquent groups, lacking more general legitimization, simply employ coercion or threat to insure compliance from the single victim.

Second, there is the persistent assumption in Wood's analysis that the stranger wishes to join the group. The need to explain assimilation of stranger to the group is present to a lesser extent in Park (1928) and Stonequist's (1937) treatment of the marginal man and represents a concern of early theorists with the problem of explaining order. What makes Wood's analysis different from the latter is that the stranger-newcomer has little to contribute by virtue of his or her unique status; the problems of adjustment to the group are assumed to be of major concern for the newcomer.

But an assumption that the offender wishes to join a group of victims is obviously inconsistent with a portrayal of violent victim/offender relationships. Violent encounters occur because the offender is taking the property of others by force or because of an interpersonal conflict. It is difficult to imagine the stranger offender desiring to join a group of which the victim is a member.

Wood's study of the newcomer is not without some positive implications for the study of stranger violence. One implication is that situational behavior involving strangers will not be understood unless we consider the values and norms held by the group and the stranger before their involvement in the situation. Thus, an explanation of homicide that relies on an escalating cycle of situationally induced threats and counter-threats must confront questions implied in Wood's analysis (Luckenbill, 1977). Not everyone who is insulted in a bar returns the insult, thus initiating a cycle with a violent outcome. Some people turn away, others joke, some get up and leave. To some extent, one must be committed to the rules of the game before it is played. Such commitment implies a congruence in values and norms between strangers at the beginning of the encounter (Wood, 1934).

Wood's discussion of the categoric motive is also relevant to our purposes. She suggests that even very superficial contacts between strangers are patterned. Simply by observation, a stranger forms or uses already formed expectations about another stranger. Such expectations serve to guide behavior in these early and perhaps conclusive encounters.

NOTES

1. Jason, Strauss, and Tyler (1983) divided homicides into primary and secondary homicides. While they cited the Parker and Smith research, they did not base their classification on relationships. A primary homicide occurred "when it was the main reason for the offender's assault; it was 'secondary' when the offender's primary intent was to commit some other crime and the homicide occurred secondary to this activity" (p. 310).

2. This chapter will use the translation provided by Kurt H. Wolff, The Sociology of Georg Simmel (1964).

3. Sirius is the brightest star in the heavens, located in the constellation Canis Major; also called the Dog Star.

4. This pithy and familiar characterization of the stranger was not used by Simmel. McLemore (1970) states that its earliest use was found in Wood (1934).

REFERENCES

Anderson, N. (1923). The hobo: The sociology of the homeless man. Chicago: University of Chicago Press.

Boskoff, A. (1972). The mosaic of sociological theory. New York: Thomas Y. Crowell.

Bureau of Justice Statistics (1982). Violent crime by strangers. Washington: U.S. Government Printing Office.

Bureau of Justice Statistics (1987). Violent crime by strangers and nonstrangers. Washington: U.S. Government Printing Office.

Cohen, L. E. & Felson, M. (1979). Social change and crime-rate trends: A routine activities approach. American Sociological Review, 44, 588-608.

Cohen, L. E. Kluegel, J. R., & Land, K. C. (1981). Social inequality and predatory criminal victimization: An exposition and test of a formal theory. American Sociological Review, 46, 505-524.

Coser, L. A. (1965). The stranger in the academy. In L. A. Coser (Ed.), Georg Simmel (pp. 29-39). Englewood Cliffs: Prentice-Hall.

Curtis, L. A. (1974). Criminal violence: National patterns and behavior. Lexington: Lexington Books.

Felson, M. & Cohen, L. E. (1980). Human ecology and crime: A routine activity approach. Human Ecology, 8, 389-406.

Freeman, C. (1975). A world full of strangers. Toronto: Bantam Books.

Githens, M. & Prestage, J. (1978). Women state legislators: Styles and priorities. Policy Studies Journal, 2, 264-270.

Hindelang, M. J., Gottfredson, M. R., & Garofalo, J. (1978). Victims of personal crime: An empirical foundation for a theory of personal victimization. Cambridge: Ballinger Publishing Co.

Jason, J., Strauss, L. T., & Tyler Jr., C. W. (1983). A comparison of primary and secondary homicides in the United States. American Journal of Epidemiology, 117, 309-319.

Levine, D. N. (1971). Georg Simmel: On individuality and social forms. Chicago: University of Chicago Press.

Levine, D. N. (1977). Simmel at a distance: On the history and systematics of the sociology of the stranger. Sociological Focus, 10, 15-29.

Levine, D. N., Carter, E. B., & Gorman, E. M. (1976a). Simmel's influence on American sociology I. American Journal of Sociology, 81, 813-845.

Levine, D. N., Carter, E. B., & Gorman, E. M. (1976b). Simmel's influence on American sociology II. American Journal of Sociology, 81, 1112-1133.

Lofland, L. H. (1973). A world of strangers: Order and action in urban public space. New York: Basic Books.

Luckenbill, D. F. (1977). Criminal homicide as a situated transaction. Social Problems, 25, 176-186.

McLemore, S. D. (1970). Simmel's 'stranger': A critique of the concept. Pacific Sociological Review, Spring, 86-94.

Meyer, J. (1928). The stranger and the city. American Journal of Sociology, 33, 476-483.

Mulvihill, D. J., & Tumin, M. M. (1969). Crimes of violence. (A Staff Report to the National Commission on the Causes and Prevention of Violence, Volume 11) Washington: U.S. Government Printing Office.

Munford, R. S., Kazer, R. S., Feldman, R. A., & Stivers, R. R. (1976). Homicide trends in Atlanta. Criminology, 14, 213-231.

National Safety Council (1972). Safety on the streets: Manual of safe procedures for women. Chicago: National Safety Council.

Park, R. E. (1928). Human migration and the marginal man. American Journal of Sociology, 33, 881-89.

Park, R. E., & Burgess, E. W. (1924). Introduction to the Science of Sociology. Chicago: University of Chicago Press.

Park, R. E., Burgess, E. W., & McKenzie, R. D. (1925). The City. Chicago: University of Chicago Press.

Parker, R. N., & Smith, M. D. (1979). Deterrence, poverty, and type of homicide. American Journal of Sociology, 85, 614-624.

Parsons, T. (1968). The structure of social action (Vol. 1). New York: Free Press.

Riedel, M., & Zahn, M. (1985). The nature and patterns of American homicide. Washington: U.S. Government Printing Office.

Riedel, M. (November, 1981). Stranger homicides in an American city. Paper presented at the meeting of the American Society of Criminology, Washington.

Sampson, R. J. (1987). Personal violence by strangers: An extension and test of predatory victimization. Journal of Criminal Law and Criminology, 78, 327-356.

Shaler, N. S. (1904). The neighbor. Boston: Houghton Mifflin.

Simmel, G. (1964). [The sociology of Georg Simmel]. (K. Wolff, Ed. and trans.). New York: Free Press.

Simmel, G. (1978). [The philosophy of money]. (T. Bottomore and D. Frisby, Eds. and trans.). London: Routledge & Kegan Paul.

Stonequist, E. (1937). The marginal man. New York: Scribner.

Tenbruck, F. H. (1965). Formal sociology. In L. A. Coser (Ed.), Georg Simmel (pp. 77-96). Englewood Cliffs: Prentice-Hall.

Thrasher, F. M. (1927). The gang. Chicago: University of Chicago Press.

Turner, R. (1964). The social context of ambition. San Francisco: Chandler Publishing Co.

Weingartner, R. H. (1959). Form and content in Simmel's philosophy of life. In K. H. Wolff (Ed.), Georg Simmel: Essays on sociology, philosophy, and aesthetics (pp. 61-99). New York: Harper and Row.

Wolfgang, M. E. (1958). Patterns in criminal homicide. Philadelphia: University of Pennsylvania Press.

Wood, M. M. (1934). The stranger: A study of social relationships. New York: Columbia University Press.

Young, P. V. (1932). The pilgrims of Russian town. Chicago: University of Chicago Press.

Zorbaugh, H. (1929). The gold coast and the slum. Chicago: University of Chicago Press.

CHAPTER 5

STRANGERS: ENCOUNTERS, LOCATIONS, AND INTERACTION

Conceptualizations of strangers provided in the previous chapter do not seem to conform to today's urban world, especially with respect to violent encounters. In considering interaction with strangers, contemporary city dwellers are not concerned with how strangers might relate to any groups to which the urban dweller might belong. The image of the stranger is one of fear and avoidance rather than one of acquaintance and understanding. Even for encounters with strangers in an urban setting where crime is not a consequence, the characterization of the stranger as a "marginal man" or a "newcomer" does not seem very appropriate.

Simmel, Park and Stonequist, and Wood did recognize, however, the importance of understanding the place of the stranger in broader society. Stranger relationships need to be explained before stranger violence because the latter emerges from the former. Stranger violence, like crime in general, develops out of existing social conditions and relationships. The present chapter not only provides a view of stranger relationships in contemporary urban settings, but shows how such relationships and settings can be brought to serve deviant and violent goals.

A PERSPECTIVE ON STRANGER
RELATIONSHIPS

Cities are pre-eminently the home of strangers. In small towns and rural areas, the stranger was regarded as an exceptional person; someone whose appearance represented a break in the social routine and someone who deserved attention. With the emergence of cities, all that changed. Where every person cannot be personally known, the stranger is the rule. Lofland (1973) characterizes the urban social situation well:

Meeting strangers was no longer rare, it was a constant occurrence; and under these circumstances, the old ways of handling them were untenable. It's one thing to kill such persons when they appear infrequently; it's another when they're continually about. It's quite possible to provide every stranger one meets with bed and board and good fellowship, but only as long as one doesn't meet too many. It's plausible to believe that the first stranger one sees is a god; it strains one's credibility to think that 100,000 gods have congregated in one place. One can take the time to interrogate the occasional stranger, but interrogating every person one meets in the street becomes a bit cumbersome. The old ways had served the people living in small personal worlds quite well; for the city dweller, however, they would not do. They required too much--psychically, temporally, and economically. The old ways worked well when the small personal group confronted the infrequent stranger. They would not work at all for the stranger in the midst of strangers. (Lofland, 1973: 12)

Given the minimal involvement of strangers with one another, the central question is how is life in a city possible? To answer this question, Lofland (1973) states that behavior among strangers is learned in much the same way that other behavior is learned. Through a continuous process of interaction in a myriad of settings, social expectations serve to guide urban dwellers in their daily dealings with strangers.

Drawing on interactionist theory, Lofland suggests that there are two modes of knowing another in social situations. Personal knowing involves knowing something about the individual's biography, however slight. Personal knowing is being able to recognize someone by name, face or by some other means; actual acquaintanceship is not necessary to know another personally. We may know Joe, my cousin Mary's friend, celebrities, or even people long dead by means other than actually meeting them. Lofland notes that biographers may come to have an extensive and intimate knowledge of their long dead subjects without ever having met them.

Categoric knowing, on the other hand, relies, as the name implies, on broad social pigeonholes:

> By categoric knowing, I refer to knowledge of another based on information about his roles or statuses, to use the standard sociological jargon. That is, one knows who the other is only in the sense that one knows he can be placed into some category or categories. One knows that the other is a policeman or a whore or a female or an American Indian or a student or a Frenchman or a king, or some combination thereof. (Lofland, 1973: 15)

According to Lofland, strangers are people who we come to know only through social categories. In addition, she adds one other criterion: the stranger must be visually available. There are several aspects to this definition that require additional discussion because the formulation is central to much of what is to follow.

Knowing Strangers Through Social Categories

Defining strangers as others who are known in terms of social categories is a useful tactic. Much of our routine daily intercourse with strangers relies on our developing social expectations and behavioral repertoires based on the social categories of the persons we encounter. It is easy to underestimate the extent to which we use social categories to type and respond to stranger-others; this process occurs so reflexively that we seldom give conscious thought to what we are doing. For those people who become particularly proficient at assessing the character and problems of a stranger on the basis of limited information, such skill can provide a source of income.

Being able to persuade a stranger that you know all about his or her personality and problems is a procedure known as "cold reading" (Hyman, 1977). Hyman indicates that the cold reader must project an air of confidence, and be prepared to characterize the stranger with general statements to which he or she can assent. Such are the techniques of successful astrologers, palm readers and fortunetellers. However, something additional is needed. The person doing a cold reading must be able to use information derived from social categories: the person's age, sex, race and appearance. Hyman suggests that the successful cold reading assumes that our problems are generated by the major transitions of birth, work, marriage, children, and old age. Hyman gives an illustration from the life of John Mulholland, a well-known magician:

The incident took place in the 1930s. A young lady in her late twenties or early thirties visited a character reader. She was wearing expensive jewelry, a wedding band, and a black dress of cheap material. The observant reader noted that she was wearing shoes which were currently being advertised for people with foot trouble. . . . By means of just these observations the reader proceeded to amaze his client with his insights. He assumed that this client came to see him, as did most of his female customers, because of a love or financial problem. The black dress and the wedding band led him to reason that her husband had died recently. The expensive jewelry suggested that she had been financially comfortable during marriage, but the cheap dress indicated that her husband's death had left her penniless. The therapeutic shoes signified that she was now standing on her feet more that she was used to, implying that she was working to support herself since her husband's death. (Hyman, 1977: 26)

To some extent, social expectations and behavior are influenced by the appearance of the other person: how he or she is dressed and groomed, for instance. But such cues are less reliable indicators of social identity for the contemporary urban dweller than they were for his counterpart in the preindustrial and early industrial city. In those settings, the manner of dress would likely be a major indicator of social class and occupation and could provide substantial information about how the person should interact with the stranger.

For contemporary urban dwellers, factors related to appearances are apt to be less important than the location of the encounter with the stranger, for two reasons. First, there now are only a few occupations where uniforms are required (police, waiters, hotel doormen, bellboys, nurses, waitresses). Second, appearances are unreliable indicators for contemporary urban dwellers because styles and types of clothing are easily reproduced and readily available. A longshoreman can look like a banker and vice versa. Some physical characteristics can also be changed easily to accommodate changing styles and trends. Initially, long hair and beards marked the appearance of the hippie, beatnik and assorted other persons largely unacceptable to the middle class. Soon, however, these hirsute fashions were modified and adopted by many of the very people who first deplored them (Lofland, 1973).

Today, a uniform signals the identity of the stranger so rapidly that interaction occurs without much else being learned. Nuns, for example, complain that if they wear traditional garb, no one ever looks at their face. When the uniform is that of a low status occupation, it relegates the person to the position of "nonperson"; he or she is interactionally "nothing but" the workman or the doorman. All of us have had the experience in restaurants of trying to locate our waiter or waitress when he or she is not at our table. We cannot find him or her among all the similarly dressed persons because we responded to the uniform and did not look at the person's face.

Among important appearential factors that serve to identify strangers is skin color. Blacks become aware of the extent to which the color of skin creates a nonperson in social settings. Ralph Ellison's novel, Invisible Man describes the condition:

> I am an invisible man. No, I am not a spook like those who haunted Edgar Allan Poe; nor am I one of your Hollywood-movie ectoplasms. I am a man of substance, of flesh and bone, fiber and liquids--and I might even be said to possess a mind. I am invisible, understand, simply because people refuse to see me. . . . Nor is my invisibility exactly a matter of biochemical accident to my epidermis. That invisibility to which I refer occurs because of a peculiar disposition of the eyes of those with whom I come in contact. A matter of the construction of their inner eyes, those eyes with which they look through their physical eyes on reality. (Ellison, 1947: 3)

In addition, those blacks in low status occupations are often required to wear uniforms. The combination of the two serves to reinforce the "nonperson" view.

Also, there are tacit rules governing the behavior of strangers in public locations. Certain people are expected to be found in certain social situations, but not in others. When individuals are unexpectedly discovered in uncommon situations, it is usually made clear they are not welcome or they are driven away. The best example of the latter is found in patterns of residential segregation. Early in his life, Malcolm X made his living by burglarizing homes in wealthy white neighborhoods, but he knew that his efforts to "case" homes as possible targets would alert the police and cause them to ask him what he was doing in the neighborhood. So he convinced two white women to get themselves invited into the homes on some pretense. Sometimes the proud homeowner would even show them around providing additional information useful in a future burglary (Malcolm X, 1966).

The location of the encounter with a stranger is a particularly important and useful cue to identity. A well-dressed middle aged male walking across a university campus is not likely to be regarded as a student. Consider the appearance of a young white male wearing a t-shirt and a pair of dirty jeans. Whether we conclude he is a drug addict, a criminal, or a college student depends very much on where we see him. If he is leaning against the side of a building in a bad section of town, the inference of drug addict or criminal would be likely. However, if we see him walking across a campus, a likely inference would be that he was a college student. In practice, of course, many more social identities than the three mentioned would be considered for imputation to the young man. In other words, while the appearance of the stranger does not vary, the imputed social identity changes according to location.

The Emphasis on Vision

As indicated earlier, Lofland included the criteria of visual availability in her definition of strangers. In other words, for persons to qualify for that title, it must be possible to observe them.

But why the emphasis on visual availability when we learn about people from a variety of senses? The sex of speakers, geographical origin and sometimes even ethnicity can be ascertained without seeing. Although other senses, such as smell, are more unreliable, sound is a useful source of input for categorizing strangers. The difference is that, unlike his small town counterpart, the urban dweller uses vision disproportionately to inform himself about others around him. As Simmel noted: "Social life in the large city as compared with the towns shows a great preponderance of occasions to see rather than to hear people" (Simmel, 1924: 360).

Vision is notably efficient; not only does it take less time, generally it covers a greater distance than other senses. Second, given the logistical and bureaucratic problems of servicing an urban population, city residents must spend much time in public space, waiting in lines, waiting to be served, and waiting for others. They may pass the time by talking to those nearby, but such conversation is apt to be with strangers, an activity not casually entered into by most urban dwellers. Usually, they remain silent and observe others.

The importance of vision is obvious when the number of signs used in a city to inform us about prescribed and proscribed behavior is compared with those in a small town. Besides clusters of street signs telling us the identity of the street, the highway, whether parking is permitted and, if so, what kind and how long, we are confronted with signs in various other locations that announce the prohibition of smoking, spitting, eating and drinking. There is apt to be a sign in restaurants that reserves the right not to serve us, and there are others that advise: "Please Pay When Served." The multitude of signs just mentioned does not, of course, include the large number that identify stores, the variety of objects sold there and their prices.

The urban dweller visiting the small town for the first time is often frustrated in efforts to find a specific person or location. Street signs are missing or damaged; house numbers are displayed inconsistently, if at all. Signs identifying the type of store are in a state of disrepair or nonexistent. Such urban amenities, which rely on vision, are not necessary where everyone is personally known. The expectation of the small town dweller is that only a few people are strangers and they can, after all, ask anyone where the person or location is that they are seeking.

TYPES OF STRANGER RELATIONSHIPS

Lofland used the term "visually available" to emphasize the interactional and processural nature of her theory. The term seems to refer to all people within the range of our vision with whom it is possible to interact. We need not interact with them, but the possibility is there. Visual availability appears to be similar to what Goffman (1963) called copresence. In public settings, people act as if they will be seen by others and will, in turn, see them. Because of this expectation, they dress and act differently from how they would look and behave in a private setting. Visual availability represented Lofland's interest in sociological possibilities: what can occur between two strangers and how their behavior can be mutually altered as a result of their encounter.

A more detailed specification of visual availability leads to the suggestion that there is more than one kind of stranger relationship. In the course of routine activities, urban dwellers do not approach others in a random fashion merely because these others are visually available; visual awareness of others is a process that occurs within the larger arena of visual availability. Approaches by and interaction with strangers are guided by social expectations and the social nature of the setting just as surely as other kinds of interaction.

There appear to be two general classes of stranger relationships. The first is called spontaneous relationships, which have an unrehearsed, immediate and mutual character about them. Strangers seem to begin interacting with one another more or less simultaneously and reflexively, often about very trivial events. For example, I may be sitting in a bar watching a sports event on television; the stranger next to me may make some comment on the skill of the players to which I respond. The other person may respond or the exchange may lapse into silence.

The second class of relationships, selective relationships, seems to take on a one-sided nature. A person shopping in a clothing store looks around for a sales clerk to provide information about an article of clothing. Spotting the clerk at the other end of the aisle, the customer approaches him or her for the needed information. All the while, the clerk may have been busy with some other task and may be unaware that he or she is the target of the stranger's approach.

Selective and spontaneous stranger relationships are made possible by serveral conditions that, loosely construed, relate to either persons or settings. Selective relationships are those in which the actor views the characteristics of another as making them available for an encounter. For example, there are occupational positions in which part of the role requires interaction with strangers. These include the wide variety of occupations such as retail sales clerks, receptionists, filling station attendants, and grocery checkers who must hold themselves open to approaches by strangers.

Goffman (1963) suggests that there are social positions that open incumbents to approaches by a wide variety of strangers. People such as police officers and priests are viewed as those toward whom strangers may extend a greeting without a request for information.

There are broad statuses that include old people and the very young which "seem to be considered so meager in sacred value that it may be thought their members have nothing to lose through face engagements, and hence can be engaged at will" (Goffman, 1963: 126). It is not uncommon for an elderly person, who may sit down to rest in a shopping mall, to often find himself or herself engaged in a conversation with a stranger. Goffman's view on the profane nature of the elderly also may well explain why situation comedies on television have recently "discovered" the elderly actor and actress, and why the dialogue of such shows is more sexually explicit than is the case with younger performers.

Children are also included by Goffman within that broad status of profane people who can be approached by strangers. While Goffman's observations may have been correct at the time they were written, today, when public sensitivity has been increased concerning the dangers of child abuse, the approach to children by strangers is viewed with caution. It remains appropriate, however, for strangers to talk to children when the children are in the presence of an adult.

Because there are bonds, albeit limited, between strangers in public settings, a stranger may approach others when in need of help or small favors such as asking for a light or information as to the location of a store. While those accosted have some obligation to respond, those doing the accosting have an obligation to choose targets who will not read the encounter as a threatening approach. Thus, a young man who approaches a young lady on a public street and asks for directions may find that he will be ignored or given very abrupt treatment.

In contrast to selective relationships, spontaneous relationships are those in which, because of the nature of the setting, actor and other are mutually open to encounters. An important basis for mutual accessibility occurs in what Goffman calls "open regions---physically bounded places where 'any' two persons, acquainted or not, have a right to initiate face engagements with each other for the purpose of extending salutations" (Goffman, 1963: 132). Such places include bars, cocktail lounges, and spectator sports arenas, to name a few. There is an obligation in these settings to respond to the initial comments of the stranger.

Parties, particularly large parties, in private homes are another instance of a setting where spontaneous relationships among strangers occur. If strangers are not introduced by the host or hostess, they may take it upon themselves to introduce themselves. Because all the members assume that the guests were invited by the host or hostess, there is a social obligation to respond reciprocally to the approach of a stranger.

The felt obligation in settings involving spontaneous relationships extends only as far as responding to the initial salutation. Encounters are easily initiated and can just as easily be ended. Such termination can range from silence after the first exchange to a thinly veiled excuse for moving to another part of the setting. Thus, a woman who no longer wants to continue the conversation in a bar with a newly met male may excuse herself to greet a newcomer, say hello to a friend, or go to the "powder room."

It is apparent that spontaneous and selective stranger relationships do not occur in social vacuums. The two types of stranger relationships differ in the approaches to another; the difference in the approaches are made possible, in part, by the nature of the setting. As Lofland (1973) has noted, location is a potent source of information in forming the expectations of strangers who are about to interact. To complete the general conceptualization of stranger relationships, the following section will consider the role of behavior settings and its relationship to the two types of stranger relationships.

LOCATIONS AND BEHAVIOR SETTINGS

Spatial dimensions are probably more important with respect to interacting with strangers than with nonstrangers because, except for categorical characteristics, little is known about the other person. Location, then becomes disproportionately important for informing our interactional expectations and imputing an identity to the stranger.

Location can be differentiated into configurations of time, space, and objects such as grocery stores, gas stations, clothing stores, parks, streets, and doctor's offices. Associated with these behavior settings are widely shared sets of beliefs about the appropriate kinds of behavior that can occur there (Barker, 1968). These standing patterns of behavior describe "what activity can take place as a matter of course and without question, and for what conduct those present will be held accountable" (Cavan, 1966: 3).

A behavior setting consists of standing patterns of behavior and milieu. The relationship that must exist between the milieu and the behavior has been described by Barker (1968) as synomorphic, meaning similar in structure. Synomorphy means that the behavior and the surrounding must be consistent with each other. For example, the boundary of a football field is the boundary of the game. The behavior that occurs in a bar is bounded by the walls and ceiling of the establishment. Synomorphy extends into the details of the setting. Roebuck and Frese (1976) in their study of an after-hours bar, for example, showed how the various behavior settings of the establishment corresponded to different types of standing patterns of behavior.

There are numerous sources of behavior-milieu synomorphy. Take physical arrangements, for example. Corridors make possible locomotion in certain directions, their narrowness make it difficult for groups of more than two or three people to meet for discussions. The presence or absence of chairs and the way they are arranged make possible certain types of interaction, but not others.

The casual observer of human behavior cannot help but be impressed with the extent to which settings impose demands that are met by appropriate behavior and how behavior can vary to match the setting. For example, two members of the same academic department may be the most bitter of enemies in their daily exchanges, resorting to every tactic to belittle and reduce one another's ability to work well. Yet, when we find the two at a cocktail party or a faculty reception a bare hour after work, they may be very sociable. Observing the latter would make the casual observer believe that, if they are not the best of friends, they are, at least, very congenial colleagues.

Some behavior settings set admission criteria that, in turn, have an influence on the kinds of standing behavior patterns that exist in the group. Thus, prisons will not admit people as permanent residents unless they have been convicted of a crime. Women's Centers admit only women who have been the subject of physical or psychological abuse.

There are also a large variety of fraternal, business, and special interest organizations that maintain the standing patterns of behavior through selection. This includes such organizations as the high school and Greek letter fraternities and sororities, Elks, Moose, and Rotary Clubs, and Veterans of Foreign Wars, to name a few. Special interest organizations cater to just about any hobby or avocational activity that can be imagined. Here, the admission criteria may be no more than an interest in an activity such as stamp collecting, amateur radio broadcasting, computing, gardening, bird watching, collecting antique automobiles, breeding dogs, whitewater canoeing, or flying airplanes.

To maintain the standing patterns of behavior, members of a group may be ejected if they do not comply with rules of the setting. People who belong to a bridge or poker group and consistently cheat may no longer find themselves welcome members. Students who do not comply with the rules of the school are expelled. Even inmates of penal institutions can be so persistently violent that they are transferred to other institutions where security arrangements are more appropriate to their behavior.

Part of the reason there is an affinity between the standing patterns of behavior and behavioral repertoires is that people discriminate and select the settings of which they wish to be a part. Unmarried women may go to a singles bar once and decide this is not a setting for them because of the behavior that is expected. Those that remain in the setting of singles bars are self-selected because of their interest in conforming to the standing patterns of behavior.

While standing patterns of behavior are widely shared they are not unchangeable. The people who support them also, over time, change them. For example, if the behavior of college students is observed when they walk between buildings on a campus, it will be noticed that most of the time their path follows the sidewalks. However, in several places, the ground will be worn bare where students cut across the grass in the interest of shortening the distance. Sometimes, after the path is well established, the university puts down a sidewalk. There are instances where university administrators constructed a new building without any joining sidewalks. After observing the pattern of traffic for a period of time, they simply instructed that sidewalks be laid down where there were well-defined footpaths. In other words, rather than the milieu defining the behavior, the behavior defined the milieu.

Behavior settings are most easily discussed when they are easily circumscribed by a physical structure. The previous discussion focused, for example, on behavior in classrooms, bars, and club meetings. The physical and social boundaries may, however, be more diffuse, as happens with encounters on a street. Barker has noted that behavior settings need only have "a precise position in space which can be designated with the degree of precision the investigator requires" (Barker, 1968: 26).

That street settings may be more diffuse than those with obvious physical boundaries has been noted by Goffman (1963). While social occasions such as weddings, a workday in the office, or a picnic are obviously bounded, a social occasion like Tuesday afternoon downtown is more diffuse. Goffman suggests that, in the latter instance, a more useful term would be "behavior setting. Diffuse social occasions can, of course, develop a structure and direction as they go along" (Goffman, 1963: 19).

All participants in a behavior setting are not equally knowledgeable of the standing behavior patterns. Thus, an elected official with high social visibility may join a men's club only to find that it has a long-standing tradition of excluding women and minorities. When this is brought to the attention of the public by an energetic media, the official may resign, claiming ignorance of the standing behavior pattern. The official claims of ignorance, assuming they are sincere, mark the difference between the perspective of a newcomer and an insider.

There is also a difference between compliance and conformity concerning standing behavior patterns. Compliance is overt conforming behavior expressed by people who have an interest in exploiting or manipulating settings in ways that are neither routine nor proper.

Sometimes the exploitation may involve the setting in behavior that is illegal. For example, where some members of an office use the setting to buy and sell cocaine and use it, the standing behavior patterns can serve as a camouflage for the illicit activity. In other instances, a person may pose as a member of the setting to learn more about the standing behavior patterns. In Alfred's (1976) study of the Church of Satan, he came to the group as an outsider and, feigning conversion, made rapid progress in the ritual and administrative hierarchy of the group. It was only near the end of his study that he told the leader of the group that it had been the object of research.

Standing patterns of behavior are shared not only by the people in the setting, but by those outside the setting as well. Urban dwellers not only develop cognitive maps of the city, but tend to "weight" their classification of various settings affectively. They classify settings as good and bad, desirable and undesirable and they tend not to go to settings where unpleasant or unwanted encounters with strangers may occur. "Biker" bars, for example, are usually avoided by the prudent urban dweller. The cognitive and affective component of behavior settings is described by John Lofland:

> Places themselves vary in the definitions accorded them by the public at large. Just as human bodies are the kinds of objects to which deviant and normal imputations can be made, so too are physical territories or places. . . . Human beings can impute to territories, somewhat independently of people, a character or identity. In this sense, pieces of land and people are much the same kinds of objects.
>
> Imputations to places imply some conception of an appropriate (even if immoral) clientele felt typically to inhabit or to frequent them. Nice places are frequented by that kind of people; crummy places are frequented by their kind of people. (Lofland, 1969: 168)

Thus, places can be used to infer purpose and place blame. For example, an offender may observe that a young woman goes home a certain time every day by using a shortcut through a badly lighted and isolated section of a public park. If she is raped in that place, there is a tendency for police and public to suggest that her behavior in going through the park was questionable. After all, a female who walks through "that area" by herself may be construed to be "asking for it," or inviting a sexual encounter.

Behavior Settings and Stranger Relationships

As the preceding section made clear, there are a vast variety of behavior settings. There appear to be two types of settings that make possible selective and spontaneous relationships: serious and unserious.

Much of what we do when we recreate and work with others can be distinguished by the anticipated consequences of our behavior. Work, because of its consequences, is one of the most important activities that occurs in serious settings. Gainful employment is fraught with serious consequences: whether we consistently report to work on time, the quality of the work we do, whether such work is completed at a rate that is expected by our supervisors, the amount of cooperation that we show in working with others, the willingness to be supervised by others in the work setting are all factors that determine whether the person is retained and promoted. Such activities make it possible for us to realize our individual potential through our work, enjoy greater prestige or greater income, or, sometimes, all three.

In her perceptive analysis of serious and unserious settings, Cavan (1966) indicated unserious settings are analogous to a "time out" in sporting events where the rules of the game are suspended while coaches talk to players, walk on the playing field, change equipment, argue, and generally do things that are not permitted during the game.

Cavan goes on to suggest that there are public settings that are unserious in nature. People who are participants in settings like bars, parties, beaches, resorts, and carnivals enter a setting where they believe that their behavior will not have consequences outside the setting.

Drawing from the writings of Huizinga and Simmel on play and sociability, Cavan (1966) and Roebuck and Frese (1976) point out that settings in bars involve a suspension of reality, a stepping out of the real world into a realm where the consequences of one's action are determined in the here and now. Unserious settings are places where differentials in social status are held in abeyance, and where people assume identities that cannot be maintained outside the setting. In contrast to work settings, unserious settings are where people have the freedom to initiate and terminate interaction with others, including strangers. In addition, the limits of acceptable behavior are broader and a larger variety of deviant behavior is acceptable.

The times of operation of serious and unserious settings generally parallel the division of most people's daily and weekly work and play activities. Serious settings occupy the daylight hours of the Monday through Friday while unserious settings are available during the evening hours and the weekends.

There are, however, many variations. Some serious settings, such as supermarkets or convenience stores, are open into the evening hours or on a twenty-four hour basis. Other serious settings, such as banks, are open during evening hours, but may limit the kinds of services available. Still others, like streets, may limit the presence of certain demographic groups, like teenagers under 16, during late evening and early morning hours.

Similarly, for unserious settings, bars and cocktail lounges may be legally open at 11:00 in the morning. Some open at that time while others wait until 5:00 in the afternoon. After-hours bars, although generally illegal, may open at 1:00 a.m. and remain open until 7:00 a.m. (Roebuck and Frese, 1976). For many play settings, when the event occurs depends on the availability of enough people to carry off the behavior involved. This ranges from a sandlot baseball game, which can occur anytime, to major league play, which usually occurs in the evening when a large audience is expected to be available.

Most of a city dweller's time is spent in serious settings. Much time is spent in the workplace where what we do has important consequences in terms of money and status. In addition, the city dweller makes use of serious settings when he or she goes to the bank for cash, buys gas for his or her car, gets it serviced or repaired, purchases food, clothing, and other services necessary to a conventional urban lifestyle. It should be no surprise that the selective relationships among strangers and the recorded robberies and robbery murder that occur in these settings are more numerous than those involving spontaneous relationships.

The lack of consequentiality that characterizes unserious settings means that interaction among strangers readily occurs. The ease of interaction that occurs there is what gives spontaneous stranger relationships their distinctive character of mutuality, improvisation, and lack of premeditation. Strangers can be approached and conversation initiated within the limits of permissible behavior. The spontaneous relationships in an unserious setting seem to flow from the setting itself. Roebuck and Frese (1976) describe how such spontaneous encounters occur:

Encounters between those not acquainted are ordinarily accomplished by remarks, queries, or declarations that actually serve as ritual forms or moves requesting conversation. Typically, a patron within conversation range of another patron with whom he desires an encounter directs toward this person casual comments about the bar, the weather, sports, music, barmaids, or cocktail waitresses. Should the approached patron respond with more that a brief nod, gesture, or verbal acknowledgement, the initiator receives cue to answer---and with this exchange an encounter begins . . . . Encounter patterns frequently consist of remark, counter remark, interchange, silence, remark, counter remark, and so on. (Roebuck and Frese, 1976: 104)

Not only does the unserious setting encourage spontaneous relationships, but the range of tolerable behavior is very wide. Both Cavan (1966) and Roebuck and Frese (1976) found that people creating scenes or spectacles or engaging in self-indulgent behavior would provoke little sanction from management or other patrons. The line would be drawn at displays of physical violence, but even there, in Cavan's research, they would be ignored if short and quickly over. Roebuck and Frese (1976) found that the tolerance for physical violence in the after-hours bar was lower because as an illegal business, the owners were fearful of attracting the attention of the police.

The consequentiality that characterizes serious settings means that instrumental and task-related activities occur there. But in these settings, strangers do not behave as automatons; they are selective in their interaction with others. They approach stock clerks to learn the location of the item they want to buy, avoid aisles in which another customer is struggling with a full cart and a rambunctious child, move past shoppers who are idly conversing or carefully inspecting merchandise, and pick check-out lines with the fewest number of customers.

Physical objects may be used as "props" to stage or invite an encounter with a stranger. Thus, the shopper whose shopping cart "accidentally" runs into another may provide the occasion for interaction. Persons shopping for groceries may feign a lack of understanding of how to select ripe fruit when an object of their attention is nearby. Women who struggle with a heavy bag of groceries or who have trouble starting their car invite the attention of a "chivalrous" male.

Props may used to "force" the attention of another stranger. In visiting a car dealer, it is only necessary to start inspecting the vehicle on display to draw the attention of the salesperson. To be served in a busy restaurant, a stranger may, after inspecting the menu and waiting an appropriate period of time, begin to slowly gather up his or her personal belongings in preparation for leaving. One then is almost assured of the attention of a waiter or waitress.

Such selective behavior in serious settings must, however, respect the nature of the setting. It is permissible to pick the shortest line at a check-out counter; it is not permissible to "jump the line" and put oneself at the head of it. It is permissible to approach a store clerk for information, but an apology is given if the clerk turns out to be another customer. "Accidents" can be arranged with grocery carts, but if the initial approach fails, it is expected that the interaction will be ended.

Unserious settings are a kind of discontinuity in the web of consequentiality; what we do there is not supposed to have effects outside the settings. Thus, people yell, scream, and curse the officials at ball games without worrying that anyone will impute an identity of violent behavior.

But even in unserious settings, consequentiality has a way of rearing its ugly head. As Cavan has pointed out, inconsequentiality in an unserious setting may be a legitimate anticipation; it is not, "so to speak, constitutionally guaranteed as an inalienable right" (Cavan, 1966: 240). The problem is that what some people regard as inconsequential behavior may not be deemed such by others. Comments or behavior that were meant by the actor to be in the spirit of the setting are given a very different meaning by others. For example, a woman may feel that she is relatively free to flirt with other males in a bar, only to find that her division of attention leads two males to quarrel over her.

Where bars are the settings for deviant or alternative lifestyles, what occurs may have very real consequences outside the setting. Cavan gives the example of the homosexual who wishes to maintain his or her heterosexual identity, but who is discovered by a coworker in a homosexual bar. If the two coworkers are later found to be in competition for the same promotion, it may be naive to expect the other to "respect the unserious definition of the bar and hence studiously . . . ignore the information . . . which he now has" (Cavan, 1966: 241).

If the activities in an unserious setting are sometimes consequential, can the activities in serious settings lack consequentiality? The answer seems to be affirmative, but such behavior occurs most often among nonstrangers. In serious settings, consequentiality is seldom unremittingly pursued. People working in offices take "breaks," time out from the work activity in which they drink coffee, flirt, tell jokes, and chat about trivial topics. Persons who work in small groups with a minimum of supervision set self-imposed breaks: one person may say, "Listen, we've been working on this problem for three hours, let's finish this part and get some coffee." Where this is agreeable, the two or three individuals sit around and do much of what others do on breaks that are permitted in more closely supervised settings.

During these break periods, what people say is evaluated expressively rather than instrumentally. Comments that might be taken as insults while people are at work are treated as jokes. During this period of inconsequentiality, there are evident changes in posture and the use of limbs: people put their feet up on desks, clean their eyeglasses, walk around, and stare out of windows, while maintaining a conversation with their coworkers.

Such expressive behavior takes place in "backstage" areas, such as employee lounges, where the coworkers are not easily observed by strangers (Goffman, 1959). The serious nature of the setting is continuously maintained by cashiers who sometimes prepare their waiting line of strangers by announcing that this "register is closing." Other times, another cashier will take over the station in an unobtrusive fashion for the person going on a break.

Finally, serious and unserious setting and their correlative stranger relationships are not only differentiated by consequentiality and time of operation, but also by the physical arrangements of the setting. Paralleling Cavan's distinction between unserious and serious setting is Sommer's (1969) distinction between sociopetal and sociofugal space. Sociopetal spatial arrangements are those that focus people toward the center and thereby bring them together. Sociofugal spatial arrangements drive people toward the periphery of an enclosed space and make interaction more difficult. In the view presented here spontaneous relationships and unserious settings tend toward sociopetal spatial arrangements while selective relationships and serious settings are sociofugal in nature. Sommer describes airline terminals as an example of sociofugal space.

Airline terminals . . . are perhaps the most sociofugal public spaces in American society. In most terminals it is virtually impossible for two people sitting down to converse comfortably for any length of time. The chairs are bolted together and arranged in rows theater-style facing the ticket counters, or arranged back-to-back, and even if they face one another they are at such distances that comfortable conversation is impossible. The motive for the sociofugal arrangements appears the same as that in hotels and other commercial places -- to drive people out of the waiting areas into cafes, bars, and shops where they will spend money. (Sommer, 1969: 122)

While the distinction between sociopetal and sociofugal spatial arrangements is useful it does seem to underestimate the interactional complexity of the behavior occurring in these settings. The classification of a setting as, for example, sociopetal may overlook the variety of interaction occurring there. Cavan (1966) found in her study of bars that the lateral arrangement of chairs at the bar was more conducive to interaction than face to face encounters available at tables.

She also found that the boundaries between people at the bar were more unclear and fluid than at a table. There were differences in the interaction between like sex pairs and mixed sex pairs with respect to the distance they kept between each other. Like sex pairs, such as two males, would begin talking with one stool between them; that pattern was usually maintained. However, if a male and female began conversing with a bar stool between them, they would soon take adjacent seats to prevent someone else from coming between them.

Similarly, Roebuck and Frese (1976), in their study of an after-hours club, found that the sociopetal space was actually composed of four different subsettings. There was, first, the bar, which was the most open of the four regions. Here, strangers could freely interact on matters of inconsequentiality. Second, there was the nightspot subsetting that consisted of tables and chairs and was primarily oriented toward heterosexual interaction on a couple basis. The third subsetting was made up of booths along one side of the bar. This secluded area was used by couples for sexual negotiation, heavy petting, and, sometimes, sexual intercourse. Across and diagonally located from the latter was the fourth subsetting. It consisted of the two "private booths" that served as home territory for a select group of "businessmen" who would drink, eat, play dice, and socialize with one another and their girl friends.

STRANGERS, DEVIANCE, AND VIOLENCE

It was suggested previously that settings and relationships are sometimes used for other than conventional purposes. Sometimes, the prototypical spontaneous relationships among strangers in unserious settings like bars are transformed into violent encounters that culminate in injury or death. In other cases, the routine selective relationships that occur among strangers in grocery stores, banks, and the variety of other serious settings suddenly become the scene for a robbery and robbery murder. Such unconventional uses extend to deviant activities that generally do not involve violence. Unserious settings may be places where prostitutes can ply their trade or where illegal enterprises can be planned. Serious settings can be used for shoplifting or "scams" and "ripoffs" by skillful consumers.

Given the conventional world of stranger interaction portrayed in the preceding sections, how does deviance and violence among strangers occur? There seem to be two general processes associated with altering conventional stranger relationships and settings to achieve a deviant goal: exploitation and confrontation. Exploitation refers to the use of settings and relationships to achieve a deviant purpose. It is "an illicit transaction in which a deviant uses stealth, trickery, or physical force to compel another person to surrender goods or services" (Best and Luckenbill, 1982: 157). While exploitation refers to the covert use of settings or relationships, confrontation refers to the defiant facing of another stranger to achieve deviant ends. In the case of confrontation, the presence or absence of audiences are an important factor in determining the deviant outcome of the encounter.

Exploitation and confrontation are interrelated in different and complex ways with stranger relationships and settings. Figure 5-1 is a classification of the possibilities. The following sections describe nonviolent instances of exploitation and confrontation among strangers. The next chapter focuses on violent forms of exploitation and confrontation.

Exploiting the Setting

Best and Luckenbill (1982) suggest that exploitation may involve coercion or surreptitious exploitation. The difference depends upon whether the target[1] is aware at some point in the transaction of the exploitation that is occurring. Obviously, a store clerk who is facing a stranger with a gun and the demand to hand over the contents of the cash drawer is aware that the setting is no longer one in which the person in front of him or her is making a routine purchase. While coercion is a component in this situation, it is also important to consider how the setting itself has been exploited before the appearance of weapons. Indeed, whether a robbery is going to be successful depends on whether the normality of the setting can be maintained until the moment of the actual robbery, as will be discussed in the next chapter.

As cell (I) in Figure 5-1 suggests, shoplifting occurs among strangers in serious settings and involves exploitation without coercion. Exploitation of the setting in shoplifting can occur with the choice of the setting. As Weiner (1970) noted in his study of a middle-class teenage shoplifter, the offender selected as a target a downtown department store where many poorer people shop. According to the offender and her friends, store detectives and clerks tend to pay less attention to clean, neat, and well-mannered teenagers in a setting where their attention is focused on poorer, more suspicious-looking shoppers.

In exploiting the serious setting, the shoplifter has to have a rudimentary awareness of the law that governs arrest in order to use the setting to conceal the theft. Thus, to effect an arrest, all behavior by the offender must be observed by store personnel from the time of the theft

Table 5-1

Deviant Use of Settings by Stranger Relationships

		Deviant Use of Settings	
		Exploitation	Confrontation
Stranger Relationships	Selective	(I) Robberies, Robb. Murders Shoplifting	(III) Consumer "Ripoffs"
	Spontaneous	(II) Prostitution, Stolen Goods	(IV) Assaults, Murders

until apprehension (Cobb, 1978). To determine whether electronic surveillance is active, a shoplifter will attempt to conceal an item in an obvious manner, discreetly replace it on the rack or counter, then retreat to a quiet corner of the store. If store detectives come running to the "scene of the crime," the thief will assume that the area is being scanned by live rather than dummy television cameras. He or she will move to another area or store.

Cameron (1964) and Cobb (1978) describe a number of methods to conceal a theft in this setting. The large shopping bag, for example, is an effective tool of the shoplifter. Not only are people carrying shopping bags a common sight in department stores, most shoppers will put the bag down by his or her feet when examining merchandise on a counter or rack. For the shoplifter, the placement of the shopping bag (most of which have open tops) affords him or her the opportunity to drop objects discreetly into the bag. Because the shoplifter will handle the merchandise until he or she believes they are not being observed, the only opportunity that store clerks or detectives have to see the offense is the split second when the object is being dropped into the shopping bag.

Team stealing is the most difficult to detect. Some members of a team draw attention to themselves while others shoplift. Cobb (1978) reports the case where nine juvenile males entered a department store. Because several had been identified by store personnel as shoplifters, additional store detectives were called. Seven store detectives observed the nine males, but when they clustered around a display, it was difficult to determine whether any stealing was occurring. As a last resort, the store detectives made their presence known in the hope of scaring the youths off. This also failed and rightly so. On another floor other members of the same team were apparently helping themselves to merchandise certain that their confederates were keeping the store detectives busy.

The preceding describes some of the techniques used without "boosters," which are special clothing or containers used to commit a theft. These include "drop bags" which are cloth bags sewn into coat linings, umbrellas with fasteners put inside to keep the ribs open so that objects may be dropped in, and "booster boxes." The latter appears to be a large box wrapped securely with string, but it is constructed so that one end can be opened and closed easily to conceal merchandise. Such devices are taken as evidence of premeditation by judges and more severe penalties are imposed. As a result, booster devices are seldom used (Cobb, 1978).

In many respects, unserious settings (Cell II) and the spontaneous stranger relationships that occur there make exploitation easy. While the focus will be on prostitution, unserious settings can serve as a clearing house for fences and information about gambling (Roebuck and Frese, 1976). Because the behavior exhibited there is inconsequential, open, and expressive, its meaning to other participants can vary enormously depending on what else is happening in the setting and the relationships among participants.

Consider flirting or coquetry, as Simmel calls it, which is a type of behavior that flourishes in unserious settings:

> The nature of feminine coquetry is to play up, alternately, allusive promises and allusive withdrawals - to attract the male but always to stop short of a decision, and to reject him but never to deprive him of all hope. The coquettish woman enormously enhances her attractiveness if she shows her consent as an almost immediate possibility but is ultimately not serious about it. Her behavior swings back and forth between "yes" and "no" without stopping at either. (Simmel, 1964: 50)

Such behavior occurs in unserious settings, but takes on a special character when it occurs between strangers. Thus, while the wife of an associate may be flirtatious, others who know the couple will take the behavior at face value in that it is behavior consistent with the setting, but without any consequences outside of it. For strangers where nothing is known about the other person outside the setting, flirting makes the perceived promise of availability a real possibility. It is just such a set of beliefs that make bars a popular place for unmarried people to meet one another.

It is a short step from viewing inconsequential behavior in unserious settings as behavior engaged as an end in itself to viewing the behavior as a means to realize some deviant purpose. In conventional bars, prostitutes may begin their encounter with a "john" by flirting with him. Once she judges that he is interested in a sexual relationship, she often indicates the underlying purpose by letting him know the price and conditions of the sexual exchange (Greenwald, 1958). Because there can be a similarity in the approach to strangers of a prostitute and a woman simply interested in a drink and a few moments of relaxation in a bar, women with conventional lifestyles take steps to avoid an imputation of being "cheap," or easily "available." For example, women are reluctant to go to an unknown bar by themselves. Even in bars that are familiar to them, they may seat themselves in a booth or at the end of the bar so as to better control their interaction with strangers.

Deviant exploitation of the setting in the form of prostitution can create difficulties for the bar owner in the form of unwanted police attention and threats to his or her liquor license. Therefore, care is taken to present an image to the outside of law-abiding behavior. Roebuck and Frese (1976) reported that illegal goods, services and overt criminal activities were prohibited in the after-hours bar studied by them. However, patrons and their observers reported meeting and dealing with bookies, fences, gambling-house operators and prostitutes.

> The point is that although the Rendezvous is sometimes used as a clearing house for criminal activities by some actors, its front must be straight. Therefore, behavior connected with criminal pursuits must be veiled there. If not, it is negatively sanctioned. (Roebuck and Frese, 1976: 131)

In giving an example of such negative sanctioning, the authors discuss the permanent ejection of a prostitute from the bar. She was told to leave and not come back not because she was soliciting business, but because she was too obvious and persistent about it.

While certain bars acquire a reputation for being a clearing house or location for deviant activities, this reputation does not necessarily involve collusion with managers and owners. For example, among the street women studied by Miller (1986), prostitutes earned a sporadic living frequenting the bars of large hotels. Sometimes, as Cavan (1966) notes, prostitutes are simply there and available. To bring the prostitute and her client into an encounter still, however, requires skillful exploitation of the setting as the following shows.

> A young man came in with two rather nicely dressed young women. He motioned them toward the bench across from the bar and then went up to the bar. When he returned, he had a drink for himself and for one of the women, but nothing for the second. The three of them sat for a few minutes talking, and then the woman with the drink wandered off. There was a man, probably in his fifties, standing a few feet away from them, for all practical purposes simply eyeing the women who were present. The young man looked over at him, said something indistinguishable to the remaining woman he was with and then went up to the older man, saying to him, "Are you busy?"
> "No."
> "Would you like to meet a girl?"

"Yes."

"Are you violent?"

"Oh, no. I'm very pleasant."

"What's your name?"

"Stan."

"Okay, Stan, wait a minute."

The young man then returned to the girl and there were a few minutes of huddled conversation between them, while Stan stood paying no attention to them, and fidgeting in what appeared to be a rather anxious manner. Every so often he would surreptitiously look over at them.

Finally the young man went over to Stan, took him by the arm and brought him over to the woman, introducing her as Louise. After the introduction, Stan said, "Let me buy you a drink." He went to the bar and came back with a drink for himself, the young man, and the woman. The young man then moved over so that Stan could sit next to the woman, but once Stan sat down, the young man disappeared. (Cavan, 1966: 202)

Confronting Strangers

Violent and property forms of deviance by strangers can involve confrontation. Confrontation occurs during a conflict with the victim or target which gives it the character of a "showdown." The cause of the dispute may be a trivial matter, but in the course of the interaction, the ego identity of the interactants becomes part of the conflict. At that point, any attempt to peacefully resolve the conflict is perceived as making one or the other of the interactants "back down" or renounce his or her initial claims.

Confrontation can occur among strangers in selective relationships and serious settings. However, what is labelled "consumer ripoffs" in cell (III) of Table 5-1 refers to fraud perpetrated by the consumer, not the producer.

There is little doubt that the vast amount of white-collar crime is committed by occupations and organizations with the hapless consumers as victims (Sutherland, 1949; Geis and Meier, 1977; Quinney, 1964). Consumers, in a kind of rearguard action, do commit crimes against corporations. In part, they rationalize their action by believing that it is a less serious crime to steal from a large organization than an individual (Smigel, 1956).

Large business organizations value their public reputation. As Brent and Braithwaite (1983) have shown, damage to this public reputation through negative publicity can be an effective punishment and deterrent to criminal behavior by large organizations. The ordinary consumer can negatively reflect on an organizational reputation in a confrontational encounter by claiming that the article purchased is not, for one reason or another, what he or she wants.

For most consumers, their behavior with store clerks in an effort to exchange or return an article and receive their money back is a routine encounter between strangers. Yet, store policies on "returns" are often abused. For example, the customer can purchase a watch that is damaged in a scuffle or an accident. He or she can then return to a store and say that the watch was not operating when he or she put it on their wrist this morning. Because of "defective workmanship," the customer wants his money back. A customer may keep an object for a long period of time, then return it with no sales slip, knowing that a store sells the particular brand. Without a sales slip, a store cannot determine with certainty when the article was purchased or even whether it was purchased from their store.

Where stores have policies that provide for exchanges and refunds without question, the encounter between the clerk and the stranger will pose no difficulties, even though the clerk may privately conclude that the store is the target of fraud. On the other hand, where a store disputes the claim of the customer that he or she is entitled to a refund, the stage is set for a confrontational encounter.

It is interesting to observe how such serious settings are arranged to manage the conflict and minimize its impact on other customers. For example, in the modern stores of large merchandising chains where refunds or exchanges are given without question, the "customer service" area is located in the front of the store, although located out of the stream of traffic. In older stores or those with more restrictive refund or exchange policies, customer service areas are located well away from the main stream of customers. Thus, if a conflict erupts, it is within earshot of fewer customers.

Because the customer is attacking the public image of the merchandising organization in this confrontation, an audience is helpful to achieve his or her ends. A loud voice is useful to attract attention in this setting. The customer may challenge the unwillingness of a store to provide a refund in a louder and louder voice. Other customers, who may be ignoring the area where returns and refunds are given, will gather to watch the encounter. Loud comments or questions that challenge the legitimacy of a store's policies or suggest that the store is questioning the character of the customer are most effective in attracting an audience: "Are you calling me a liar?" "Now that you have my money, you don't give a damn about service!" "And I say that the merchandise was defective when I bought it!"

When the confrontation occurs also has an impact on its consequences. The customer is more likely to effect a disputed exchange or refund when more people are available as a possible audience. Thus, a confrontation may be more effective if conducted in the early evening when shopping mall stores are busy, on weekends, or after Christmas.

Such encounters are effective not only because of a larger number of people, but also because a prolonged conflict will slow down the number of people who can be served. Customers who have to wait longer because of a confrontation between another customer and the store are, at the very least, likely to be more impatient and surly when they have to interact with store employees.

Organizations also manage these confrontations by recognizing that a conflict cannot be escalated if the other actor does not respond aggressively. Thus, clerical and managerial personnel are instructed to respond in a calm, quiet, and helpful manner, even when they are subject to verbal abuse by the customer. To do otherwise would only serve to escalate the conflict.

Another type of organization that is vulnerable to consumer ripoffs are large hotels. They are particularly vulnerable to confrontations because they are captured by the serious setting. Disputed claims about lost reservations, room mixups, etc., occur at the front desk in the presence of people waiting to register; there are no "customer service" areas. Thus, disputes are resolved in favor of the customer as quickly as possible.

It is because large organizations develop detailed policies regarding consumer complaints that such encounters rarely escalate to violence. However, when such a possibility appears, security people are readily available. They, in turn, routinely coordinate their efforts with metropolitan law enforcement agencies.

Intentional and repetitive manipulations of serious settings by confrontations between strangers are probably only done infrequently by a given stranger. Confrontations of this type are effective only if the target believes in the legitimate identity of the stranger. If the offender's behavior was to become a frequent occurrence, it probably would result in an organization calling their security personnel before the confrontation got underway. Limiting the number of confrontations per stranger per store does not, however, mean that members of the public do not engage in such behavior in many different settings.

On the one hand, it may be surmised that, given the liberal exchange and refund policies of many stores, the typical consumer is honest and forthright in his or her disputes. On the other hand, given the value placed on their reputation, stores may view fraudulent returns and exchanges in the same way they view employee theft and shoplifting. It is a cost of doing business that is passed on to the consumer, particularly because it may be impossible to distinguish fraudulent claims from legitimate ones.

The final cell (IV) refers to violent acts that occur among strangers spontaneously interacting in unserious settings. What distinguishes cell (IV) from cell (III) in Table 5-1 is the lack of selectiveness that occurs in the latter. Violent encounters among strangers in unserious settings appear to simply evolve in the setting. The culmination of such interaction may be physical injury or murder.

NOTES

1. Best and Luckenbill distinguish between the victim and the target of
    deviant exploitation. "The target is the person with whom the
    person interacts whereas the victim bears the loss." (p. 157) While
    this is a useful distinction in discussing robbery and shoplifting, it
    does not hold for robbery murders where the victim is both a target
    and a victim. Further, for deviance like prostitution, and drug use,
    it is difficult to determine who is the victim. Except where the
    other person is clearly the victim, the term "target" is used.

REFERENCES

Alfred, R. (1976). The church of Satan. In C. Glock and R. Bellah (Eds.), The new religious consciousness. Berkeley: University of California Press.

Barker, R. G. (1968). Ecological psychology: Concepts and methods for studying the environment of human behavior. Stanford: Stanford University Press.

Best, J. & Luckenbill, D. F. (1982). Organizing deviance. Englewood Cliffs: Prentice-Hall.

Brent, F. & Braithwaite, J. (1983). The impact of publicity on corporate offenders. Albany: State University of New York Press.

Cameron, M. O. (1964). The booster and the snitch: Department store shoplifting. New York: The Free Press.

Cavan, S. (1966). Liquor license: An ethnography of bar behavior. Chicago: Aldine.

Cobb, W. E. (1978). Shoplifting. In L. D. Savitz and N. Johnson (Eds.) Crime in society. (pp. 923-930). New York: John Wiley.

Ellison, R. (1947) Invisible man. New York: Random House.

Geis, G. & Meier, R. F. (1977). White collar crime: Offenses in business, politics, and the professions. New York: The Free Press.

Goffman, E. (1959). Presentation of self in everyday life. Garden City, New York: Doubleday.

Goffman, E. (1963). Behavior in public places: Notes on the social organization of gatherings. New York: The Free Press.

Greenwald, H. (1958). The call girl: A social and psychoanalytic study. New York: Ballantine Books.

Hyman, R. (1977). "Cold reading": How to convince strangers that you know all about them. The Zetetic, Spring/Summer, 18-37.

Lofland, J. (1969). Deviance and identity. Englewood Cliffs: Prentice-Hall.

Lofland, L. H. (1973). A world of strangers: Order and action in urban public space. New York: Basic Books.

Miller, E. M. (1986). Street women. Philadelphia: Temple University Press.

Quinney, R. (1964). The study of white collar crime: Toward a reorientation of theory and research. Journal of Criminal Law, Criminology, and Police Science, 55, 208-214.

Roebuck, J. B. & Frese, W. (1976). The Rendezvous: A case study of an after-hours club. New York: The Free Press.

Simmel, G. (1924). Sociology of the senses: Visual interaction. In R. E. Park and E. W. Burgess (Eds.), Introduction to the science of sociology. Chicago: University of Chicago Press.

Simmel, G. (1964). The sociology of Georg Simmel (K. Wolff, Ed. and Trans.). New York: Free Press. (Original work published, 1950).

Smigel, E. O. (1956). Public attitudes toward stealing as related to the size of the victim organization. American Sociological Review, 21, 320-327.

Sommer, R. (1969). Personal space: The behavioral basis of design. Englewood Cliffs: Prentice-Hall.

Sutherland, E. H. (1949) White collar crime. New York: Holt, Rinehart & Winston.

Weiner, N. L. (1970). The teen-age shoplifter: A microcosmic view of middle class delinquency. In J. D. Douglas (Ed.), Observations of deviance. (pp. 213-217). New York: Random House.

X, M. (1966) The autobiography of Malcolm X. New York: Grove Press, 1966.

CHAPTER 6

VIOLENCE AMONG STRANGERS

This chapter will consider two categories of stranger violence. In the first category, serious settings are exploited by selective relationships among strangers. Crimes include rapes, robberies, and robbery murders, although the focus will be on robberies and robbery murders.

The second category focuses on violent stranger confrontations in unserious settings. These include encounters in which injuries occur and those where murder is the final outcome.

There are several characteristics that distinguish exploitative and confrontational stranger violence. First, in the cases of robberies and robbery murders, planning is involved, although it may vary from a few minutes to years (Walsh, 1986). This includes selection of the site, time of the robbery, and evaluation of elements in the setting itself. In confrontational violence, there appears to be little planning. What drives these confrontations in a patterned way is the emotional involvement of the interactants.

Second, because exploitative violence occurs in serious settings, many of the people in the setting have positional characteristics that make them open to interaction. Such characteristics provide additional sources of information that need to be taken into account when planning the robbery. On the other hand, while unserious settings do contain people with positional characteristics (bartenders, waitresses), most of the interaction occurs spontaneously among the setting's clientele. Given these circumstances, information about the other stranger is gained through interaction before and during the conflict.

Third, for robberies and robbery murder, redefinition of the situation occurs at or near the beginning of the encounter. Typically, such redefinition begins with a threat to injure other people in the setting. With assaults and murders in unserious settings, redefinition develops out of the interaction of the two strangers. Threats of injury and death occur much later in the encounter.

Fourth, the presence of audiences or third parties, other people observing the event who may become involved, is an element to be taken into account in planning exploitative violence. In a robbery, it is necessary to consider how they can be controlled or eliminated, i.e., executing the robbery when only store personnel are present. In confrontational violence between strangers, audiences may play an instigating or supporting role in the violence.

EXPLOITATIVE VIOLENCE: ROBBERIES AND ROBBERY MURDER

Behavior patterns in serious settings are organized around the accomplishment of a task between two strangers engaged in an encounter. The customer approaches a clerk, places the object to be purchased before him or her and indicates he or she would like to buy it. The clerk checks the price, registers the sale, and gives the customer his or her change and receipt. In such a simple and routine exchange, there is a reciprocity built upon mutual expectations that allows an encounter to go forward with a minimum of conflict. Further, these expectations guide our behavior so completely that we are generally only dimly aware of the myriad rules that guide an encounter. Like the professional athlete who makes complex physical behavior "look easy," we interact with such facility and ease that we are seldom aware of how much learning and experience a routine encounter requires. To discover otherwise, we have only to look at small children making their first purchase or observe the efforts of people socialized in other countries and cultures to understand how difficult it is to learn not only the obvious behavior patterns, but also those that are expressed by body language, gestures, slang, and silence.

Imagine, if you will, what can occur if those engaged in routine interaction are wrenched from their placid exchange by the sudden appearance of an individual with a gun threatening their life if they do not comply with his or her demands. It is precisely because we are so entrenched in the expectations that guide routine activity that the onset of a robbery shocks and surprises the victim. Shock, surprise, and a state of disbelief is a common characteristic of victims. The emotional state of the victim is often shown by their initial responses: "Are you serious?" "What are you trying to do?"

The following example from Lejeune and Alex's research on muggings indicates how a victim can persist in maintaining a conventional definition of an offender's behavior. It was only when the victim saw the knife that he redefined the initial request.

When we started getting off the elevator he turned around and he said: "Give me ten dollars." I thought he wanted to borrow ten dollars. He said, "I don't want any trouble. Give me ten dollars." And I looked him up and down, and I see he has a knife in his hand. So I didn't let myself get knifed. I gave him the ten dollars and he got off. (Lejeune and Alex, 1973: 267)

Unsympathetic to his or her endeavors as we may be, completing a robbery places a heavy burden on the offender. Unlike violence that involves friends and acquaintances, the stranger offender knows virtually nothing about the victim except what he or she can glean from his or her categorical characteristics. Further, while the stranger offender may be familiar with the setting, to exploit it, he or she must redefine it as a robbery site, being concerned with entrances, exits, and spatial arrangements within the setting. All of the latter must, of course, be integrated with considerations as to the best time to stage the encounter.

The latter means that the offender must convince the victim that (a) he or she is serious - this is indeed a robbery, and (b) control the victim's behavior and other elements in the setting so that the robbery can be successfully completed. The fact that victims and offenders know very little about each other increases the possibility of unpredictable behavior which may be perceived by the offender as a loss of control. Such circumstances are particularly likely to result in robbery murder.

Analyses of the interaction of robberies and felony murders agree that it is a patterned process, but disagree on the number of stages involved (Luckenbill, 1981; Letkeman, 1973; Lorenz Dietz, 1983; Lejeune, 1977; Walsh, 1986). Luckenbill, for example, finds four distinct interactional stages to a robbery. Lejeune, in studying muggings, found two such stages while Lorenz Dietz found three stages in studying felony murders. The present exposition follows a classification similar to that proposed by Lorenz Dietz: (1) planning the event; (2) encounter with the victim(s); (3) the aftermath. Because our interest is primarily in how strangers approach one another, the focus will be on the first two stages.

PLANNING THE EVENT

There are three characteristics associated with the planning of robberies and robbery murders. First, the time used in planning varies substantially. In general, it is greatest for bank robberies and other relatively invulnerable targets and shortest for "opportunistic" robberies and muggings. In addition, there is substantial variation among offenders concerning a particular type of target.

Second, most robberies are group-oriented activities. The group orientation is important for several reasons. Practically, the implementing of the robbery is sufficiently complex that it requires the efforts of more than one person. In addition, a group orientation is needed by the offenders to provide emotional and social support. Finally, the presence of more than one individual in robbery encounters helps offenders to impose a redefinition of the setting from a conventional to a robbery one.

Third, before the robbery definition can be imposed on the victim, it is developed by the offenders. This includes "casing" the target to assess its value as a robbery target, determining how the target should be approached, which tasks should be performed by which persons during the actual occurrence, and the determination of an escape route.

Variation in the Amount of Time

The amount of time given to the planning of a robbery varies from a few minutes to years. Walsh (1986) interviewed 69 English prison inmates whose most recent offense was robbery. Of the 69 inmates, 36 indicated they had planned their robbery while 33 stated that they did not. Of course, as Walsh notes, "since no one wants to admit that they planned and failed, possibly more of the 'unplanned' robberies (n = 33) were in fact planned" (Walsh, 1986: 69).

Among the 36 planned robberies, 25 percent involved planning for "months" and "years," 42 percent planned for "weeks" or "days," and 19 percent planned for "hours" and "minutes." Four offenders indicated that the amount of time spent planning "varies" and one offender acted on plans that had been provided (Walsh, 1986). For the felony homicides investigated by Lorenz Dietz (1983), the plans were executed within forty-eight hours.

Muggings[1] probably require the least amount of planning time. Lejeune's interviews with a sample of New York muggers suggest that planning occurs on an "emergent basis."

> Such particulars as the neighborhood in which he [the offender] hangs out, the time of day, the immediate availability of associates judged capable of assisting in the take off, the characteristics of vulnerable strangers, and the ecological and architectural features of the area that provide cover and getaway opportunities are largely attended to on an emergent basis. Most of the time these and other elements are "pieced together" in the form of a loose plan, subject to modification and improvisations as the action develops. Thus, while there is significant variation among respondents' typical procedures, the mugging is usually planned, unlike the bank robbery, some burglaries, and other more skilled utilitarian crimes, . . . immediately before its occurrence. (Lejeune, 1977: 127-128)

The emergent character of muggings serves to illustrate how a violent encounter between strangers is rooted in routine behavior and expectations about the victim. Robberies occur because offenders can "count on" the routine behavior of others. Where there is some reason that the victim does not act in a typical fashion, including appropriate caution with strangers, there may be a higher risk of victimization. Persons who are mentally disorganized for a variety of reasons may communicate that to their offender and increase their risk of victimization as the case below suggests.

> Wally Madison, an 88-year-old-white retired man who lived in a nursing home became disoriented while walking home from the drug store one day. He made a fatal mistake when he stopped to ask three young black males for directions. They hit him on the head with a pipe and made him walk with them to an abandoned brewery. Once inside they made him strip, locked him inside a wooden cabinet, started a fire underneath it, and then fled with the money he had just received from cashing his Social Security check. The victim was found several days later by some men who were exploring the building. His death was caused by trauma to the head and/or burns.

For robberies involving commercial targets, the planning of a robbery may vary from a drive around the block to "case a joint" to a complex set of plans (Einstadter, 1969). The case given below, which also resulted in murder, is typical of the planning involved.

Two black male offenders, aged 17 and 19, had been gambling and one offender had lost all his money. The two offenders drove around looking for a gas station to rob. They finally settled on a small grocery store which they "cased." They returned later and one offender entered the store. According to two customers who witnessed the event, the offender took the victim, the store manager, to the rear of the store. Two shots were fired. The offender walked past the customers and left in the car. The victim died of gunshot wounds to the neck. The two customers obtained the license of the car and called police.

Variations in planning time overlap the different types of robberies. While muggings usually involve very little time, Lejeune (1977) gives the example of one mugging where the victim was observed for two weeks before he was robbed. For commercial targets, variation in planning corresponds to the style of robbery. "Ambush" robberies involve very little planning because the success of the robbery turns primarily on surprising the victim. At the other extreme, there are bank and payroll robberies that require a great deal of planning (Letkeman, 1973).

Group Oriented Activity

Robberies and robbery murders, particularly against commercial rather than personal targets, typically involve more than a single offender. Zimring and Zuehl (1986) found that between 33 percent and 38 percent of the robberies, robberies with injury, and robbery killings involved two offenders. About one third of the latter involved one offender and about a third involved more than two offenders. Where the robbery occurs with more than one offender, police and witness descriptions give the appearance of a well-organized and integrated group. They appear at the robbery site, dominate the setting, control the victims, take the money, and leave within a few minutes.

Although the robbery group's performance bespeaks a high degree of integration and organization, it is largely limited to the setting for the immediate purpose at hand---the acquisition of money. For example, individuals are not limited to specific roles for every offense. There is variation from one robbery event to another depending on who is available, interested, what kinds of skills he or she has, and whether they are trusted by others. The kinds of group interaction that occur at this stage are evident from the comments of one of Einstadter's offenders.

For one reason, I wasn't going in, [participate in the robbery] that was the first reason. I told them that, but they wanted me to go in. Then they got talking about that he (another person) was going to drive the car because one of them couldn't see good, and the second one, he's so damn nervous he'd probably take the key out and put it in his pocket and then couldn't find the key. We didn't think he would keep his head cool enough to stay in the car listening to the radio calls come in, especially if one came in that said there was a robbery in progress. Then we didn't know how to trust the fourth guy that just came in; we didn't know whether he might run off and leave all of us, if all three of us went in. He probably wasn't going to do it, but they were considering it. Well, anyway, it all boiled down to that I should be driving the car because I don't get excited and I drive well. (Einstadter, 1969: 73)

The type of specialization that is required in a robbery is not a strict specialization; rather it is thought of as "having a line": a generalized work preference with a repertoire of skills that can be adapted to various kinds of crime according to the demands of practicality, economics and opportunity (Letkeman, 1973). Offenders may engage in "ambush" or "opportunistic" kinds of robbery to support themselves while planning a more elaborate one. If the target is sufficiently important to the offender, he or she may be willing to play a role not directly related to his "line." Thus, a safecracker may take on another kind of target if it is believed the latter target will provide a lucrative return.

A major requirement of a robbery group is for one or more of the group to be able to create a state of fear in the victim. Lejeune (1977) suggests that the very young work in groups because the presence of their numbers can compensate for individual inability to inspire fear in their victim. Females almost always team up with males and white muggers may team up with black muggers because pre-existing racial fears of the white victim will give greater credence to the threats of the offenders.

Where commercial targets are concerned, one member of the team is selected to inspire terror in the victim. As Walsh (1986) has indicated, such members must be large, well built and convey a willingness to use violence. It is possible that such people are more important among English robbers than American because the former more often use weapons other than handguns. When English robbers do use handguns, they are frequently unloaded or replicas of weapons.

Another function of the robbery group is to reduce the anxiety and fear through interaction. Before a robbery, the fear and anxiety level of offenders is very high, which is probably due more to a recognition of the tenuousness of the setting and possible failure than fear of the police.

Lejeune (1977) suggests that the would-be mugger manages his or her fear in one of two ways. First, the more often the offense occurs, the less anxiety is experienced; normalization of the act by simple frequency serves to reduce the fear.

Second, mugging is a group activity that occurs with the urging and support of peers. The presence of the group means that the act is highly observable; this, in turn, means that any outward expressions of fear must be curbed.   At the same time, the presence of others encourages expressions of bravado. But this bravado fulfills other functions; as more and more offenses are committed, the group-supported bravado acts to minimize the perceived risks of the crime. By reducing the awareness of danger, the situation becomes normalized (Lejeune, 1977).

While a group is needed to control the setting in a robbery, the nature of the group can serve to depersonalize the interaction in the setting. Lorenz Dietz (1983) points out that robbery is a conflict, a power struggle between "us" and "them" rather than "you" and "me." Such depersonalization not only encourages an instrumental view of the robbery victim, but makes murder in those settings an impersonal outcome of the conflict.

Observing and Interpreting the Setting

In planning a robbery the goal is to preserve the conventional serious nature of the setting until the actual moment of the robbery. Preserving the conventional setting serves to prevent the victims from alerting the police or the police observing some of the early stages of the robbery on their own.

Such preservation has two aspects. First, information about events that are exterior and prior to the robbery setting must be kept from police and victims. Second, information about events occurring in the setting that are relevant to the execution of the robbery must be kept secret.

In the first category, a team must be assembled and discuss the robbery location. Team members take pains to interact in conventional ways in conventional settings. Thus, a robbery may be discussed while driving around or while having drinks at a bar. Robberies are sometimes planned in prison where authorities are generally unable to control the interaction even though they may know what is being discussed (Walsh, 1986).

Besides assigning drivers, secret plans must be made for transportation to and from the setting. A typical pattern is to steal a car shortly before the robbery, drive it away from the location after the offense, then abandon it. Another less frequent pattern is to "steal" the car from someone who the offenders know and trust. This person is instructed not to report the car as stolen until after the robbery has occurred; this removes suspicion from the car owner and protects the offenders (Letkeman, 1973).

The location of the target is an important exterior planning consideration. For example, banks located on street corners offer better opportunities with respect to getaways. Similarly, the modern trend toward low counters without glass partitions makes it easy for an offender to jump over the counter (Letkeman, 1973). It is also necessary to consider where the getaway car can be parked without suspicion at the beginning of the robbery and for rapid departure after the event.

Knowledge about the location and type of alarms is necessary for a successful robbery. Some of this information will come from "leaksmen," people who deliberately or inadvertently provide information to the offenders about the target. Walsh (1986) found that many of the offenders he studied were not only technically knowledgeable about alarms and locks, but that much of their information was current.

There are also the obvious considerations concerning the time of the offense. Robbery groups attempt to learn what days the target is apt to have a large amount of cash on hand, such as paydays or shortly after a payroll delivery. Robbery groups also prefer to attack a target when there are few people in the setting to minimize the problem of controlling victims.

Finally, as part of exterior planning, decisions need to be made regarding how the target should be approached and who should do it. Sometimes, the categorical characteristics of the stranger are important in gaining access. Lorenz Dietz gives the case of a group who planned to rob a house where illegal drugs were being sold. They concluded that the only way to gain access was to send a woman because "Hey, you won't have any problem about getting in there 'cause that dopeman--- he let any woman in" (Lorenz Dietz, 1983: 58).

In planning a robbery, the interior of the setting must be observed and interpreted by members of the robbery group. Such behavior requires one or more offenders to "fit in" in such a way that his or her presence is part of the taken-for-granted behavior of a serious setting. "Casing" a setting involves a sophisticated set of perceptual skills; the offender must be able to interpret the setting as a robbery target. In short, he or she must understand how conventional settings can be exploited for violent goals.

Many of these skills are learned while in prison and, indeed, many times the information needed about a robbery site may be obtained from another inmate.   For example, one offender learned from another offender who had worked as a delivery boy for a company that they regularly kept large amounts of drugs on the premises that could readily be converted to cash.

Being able to see a setting as a location for a robbery may amount to nothing more than paying attention to the conversation of others when they talk about what they consider to be the routine activities of their job. Letkeman (1973) gives the example of one offender who learned that a company kept a large amount of cash on the premises from the incidental remarks of his girlfriend who worked there.

Other times, the offender must place himself or herself in the setting, but do it in such a way as to make their behavior appear to be part of the routine. Thus, an offender may go into a store and pay for his or her purchase with a hundred dollar bill. By observing where the clerk goes to get the change, the offender is able to ascertain the location of the safe.

Where alarms cannot be disabled in advance, robbery groups learn the location of the manager relative to his and others' access to alarm buttons. Offenders also take into account the categorical characteristics of the manager and person they must confront to determine the kind of resistance that might be encountered. In responding to the question about what a robber looks for in a manager, one robber indicated:

> Well, usually if he's middle-aged, he's usually pretty calm. They don't have a tendency to rush you. They'd be well versed, that is--- if they've held up, just do as you're told and nobody will get hurt. Sometimes you get these young managers in their late twenties or early thirties. And he figures, "Well, maybe I'm a judo expert and maybe I can catch this guy." You never know. But the older they are they seem to be more stable, more reliable. They're not too anxious to finish up on the flat, you know what I mean. They're quite reliable, you see.   They're middle-aged and they figure they've got a family, and after all, the money is insured, so why

should he step out, you know what I mean. That's what we have a law for. (Letkeman, 1973: 154)

Evaluation of a robbery location occurs right up to the moment of the event. A robbery may be aborted at the last moment if there are suspicious variations from routine arrangements. The use of the "incongruity principle" is indicated by one of Letkeman's respondents who entered a bank with the intent of robbing it. He noticed a man behind the counter standing with one foot on a chair and his arms folded. The offender left without committing the robbery convinced the man was a cop. The respondent said that a bank manager may sit on a table with his feet hanging down or have his feet on a desk, but "he will never stand with one foot on a chair." (Letkeman, 1973: 149)

It is difficult to assess to what extent elaborate planning occurs and the extent to which it contributes to a successful robbery. First, robbery encounters are much too complex to be able to anticipate in the detail that would make elaborate planning worthwhile. The most effective planning seems to center on the approach to the target, the escape route, and the technological problems of locks and alarms. It is no coincidence that the latter elements involve the most predictability, but even these cannot be anticipated with certainty. For example, a carefully planned robbery may have to be postponed because the appropriate parking space near the target is taken. The alternatives are to double park, park too far from the target, or drive around the block until a parking space becomes available (Letkeman, 1973).

Second, it is difficult to understand how plans can be carried out, assuming they exist, when a large proportion of robbers are drunk, drugged, or both. Walsh (1986) found that 48 percent of the 69 cases on which he had information about offenders indicated that they were drunk or drugged at the time of the offense. Among robberies that claimed to be planned, 75 percent of the offenders were sober. For the opportunistic robbers, the proportions were almost reversed: only 27 percent of the offenders claimed to be sober.

ENCOUNTER WITH THE VICTIMS: AN UNEXPECTED EVENT

In confronting their victims, robbery offenders have two major tasks. They must redefine the setting from one of routine activities to one in which a transfer of property is to occur under threat. In addition, they must control the victims during this process. Whether it involves reorienting the interaction of victims and offenders and "transforming their interaction to a common robbery frame" (Luckenbill, 1981: 31), "denormalizing" the setting for victims (Lejeune, 1977: 137), or "declaring the crime" (Katz, 1988), the consequences are similar. Even as offenders attempt to define the setting as normal for themselves, they are redefining it for the victim.

Ironically, the very elements that have made the robbery approach successful to the point of initiation are the ones that are essential to alter if the definition of the setting as one acceptable to robbery is to succeed. Elements in the setting and behavior that served as camouflage are the very ones that must be given a radically new meaning for the robbery to continue to completion. Thus, what is a benign, even a boring work setting, is now a dangerous one.

The process begins by taking the victims by surprise. As one of Letkeman's respondents noted, "We don't just walk in there and say, 'Well, this is a holdup, hand over the money.' We give a good bellow when we walk in." Another respondent put it more simply: "The door would fly open and the people inside, they freeze" (Letkeman, 1973: 108, 110).

The fear and momentary paralysis that follows is important because it gives the offenders the opportunity to seize the initiative and begin to redefine the behavior that is expected in the setting. Thus, in payroll and bank robberies, the hesitation of the victims gives offenders enough time to assume their positions and back personnel away from their stations before they regain their composure and push an alarm button.

Further redefinition of the setting occurs as offenders violate the conditions of conventional serious settings. The distinctions between "front" and "back" regions are no longer applicable as offenders leap over counters, hold clerks at bay, and empty cash drawers. Persons in the setting who are ordinarily accorded deference are shoved, jostled, and threatened as readily as any other person in the setting. Even the behavior of bystanders is exploited in ways that are consistent with the new demands of the setting. Customers are forced into a position of helplessness by being made to lie, face down, on the floor.

Threats, Weapons, and Force

The force of threat[2] is a central element in redefining the setting and controlling victims. Lacking a credible threat, the offenders will be unable to convince the victims to surrender their goods. For our purposes, the threat of force is "a configuration of physical and symbolic gestures which informs the target that failure to comply with a directive will bring the infliction of death or injury" (Luckenbill, 1980: 364). Threats are supported by weapons that include firearms, knifes, clubs, and the use of fists or feet.

What is essential at the outset is that it be clear to the people in the robbery setting that violence will be used unless there is compliance. The ability to create high-intensity terror seems to be more important to the English robbers studied by Walsh (1986) probably because they expressed reluctance to use the means of violence available to them. In other words, if a threat was sufficiently believable, the victims could be controlled without the use of violence.

The type of weapon also plays a role in the viability of the threat. Cook (1982) has suggested that the proportion of robberies committed with a gun is inversely related to the vulnerability of the victim. The characteristics of the gun make it distinct and superior from other types of weapons.

A gun has several characteristics that make it superior to other readily available weapons for use in violent crime. Even in the hand of a weak and unskilled assailant, a gun can be used to kill. The killing can be accomplished from a distance without much risk of effective counterattack by the victim, and the killing can be completed quickly, without sustained effort, and in a relatively "impersonal" fashion. Furthermore, because everyone knows that a gun has these attributes, the mere display of a gun communicates a highly effective threat. (Cook, 1982: 247)

Zimring and Zuehl (1986) found that 67 percent of the commercial robberies used a gun while only 39 percent of the street robberies used the latter weapon. Muggers do not attack with machine guns and bank robbers do not approach their target with clubs.

In getting victims to accept a redefinition of the setting and comply with the directives of the offender, force sometimes must be used. Whether and how much force is used depends upon the perceived credibility of the threat, the response of the victim, and the importance of the victim to the completion of the offense.

It is useful to distinguish between preemptive and reactive use of force in robberies (Lejeune, 1977). Given the success of a gun as a threat, unarmed robberies pose a greater problem with respect to controlling victims and getting them to accept the robbery definition of the setting. As one robbery offender notes:

> Now, if some guy came up to me and said, "Give me your money," and all he's got is a tire iron, I'd probably beat the hell out of him. If all you got is an iron or something like that, he'd probably just laugh at you." (Luckenbill, 1980: 367)

Preemptive force is used when the offender wants to define the robbery setting quickly and convincingly. Hitting, pushing, shoving, and slapping is a way to let the victim know that the offender is serious about the robbery. Such tactics appear to be frequent in unarmed robberies. Block and Skogan (1984) in their study of stranger victimizations found that 70 percent of unarmed robberies in the National Crime Survey involved an actual attack, while only 26 percent of the armed robberies involved an attack on the victim.

Sometimes, preemptive force is used when the offender believes he or she is unable to control the victim in any other way. For example, Lejeune (1977) gives the case of a male mugger who attacked and subdued an unsuspecting victim before robbing him because the victim was a much larger male than the offender.

Lejeune also found that younger or less experienced muggers were more likely to use preemptive force in a robbery. Because these muggers have not yet learned the most effective use of force, the tendency is to minimize the risk by using more force than would be perceived as necessary by more experienced offenders.

The reactive use of force occurs when the offender fails to obtain or loses control over the victim. Those who do not respond to the initial threats of the offender are perceived as resisting and thereby provide a justification for violent treatment. In other cases, the victim may initially comply, but at some crucial stage in the interaction refuse to continue. Such lack of cooperation justifies the use of additional force. Finally, rather than passively resisting, the victim may attempt to attack the offender in an effort to end the robbery. This also can result in the use of force by the offender, injury and possibly death for the victim.

How force will be used also depends on the anticipated role of the victim. In his discussion of the use of force, Luckenbill (1980) indicates that in some robberies, the victim is needed to participate in the robbery. For example, if the offender needs to know the location of the money or the combination of the safe, he or she may use enough force to convince the victim of the seriousness of his or her purpose, but not so much as to incapacitate him or her.

THE RELATIONSHIP BETWEEN ROBBERY AND ROBBERY MURDER

If the view is held that murder develops out of the interaction of the robbery setting, then robbery murders are never planned. As noted in an early chapter, they are events "which somehow progressed beyond the degree of harm intended by the offender" (Block, 1977: 10).

It does appear, however, that some robbery murders are planned. In studying felony murders, Lorenz Dietz (1983) found that murder was agreed on in the planning stages because the robbery was secondary to an execution, the offenders feared counterattacks or because of victim resistance. The fear of counterattack meant that the victim or victims were murdered because the offenders were known to them or because failure to murder them would lead to reprisals. The latter was the expectation in dope house or gangland style robberies. Victims were murdered when it was perceived that their resistance endangered the group members or prevented them from getting away.

Except for robberies that are secondary to executions and robbery murders that occur because of a fear of counterattacks, the current research does not indicate the extent to which serious settings are exploited for planned robbery murders. Cook (1980) has indicated that a large number of robbery murders show no apparent indication of victim resistance, but it does not necessarily follow that these murders were planned before the encounter.

For thirty cases of robbery murder in Miami and Dade county for 1976 and 1977, Cook found that twenty, or two thirds, showed no apparent victim resistance. Using the same kind of information from Atlanta, Cook found that twelve of the nineteen cases showed "a sustained intent to kill"; only three showed any victim resistance.

It might be expected that a robbery in which there were several offenders and few victims would involve a lower risk of injury because the victims would be easier to control without violence. The opposite tends to be true. Citing some earlier research in the District of Columbia, Cook (1980) reported that the likelihood of violent attack and victim injury increased with an increase in the number of offenders.

It is criminological truism that resistance by the victim during a robbery is likely to result in injury or death to the victim. For example, in their study of personal victimization, Hindelang, Gottfredson, and Garofalo found a consistent inverse relationship between loss of property and injury. Those victims who attacked the offender were likely to retain their property, but were likely to be injured while those who did not resist lost their property, but were not injured. The optimal strategy is clear, according to the authors: "give up the property and refrain from attacking the offender" (Hindelang, Garofalo, and Gottfredson, 1978: 62).

Such views are widely accepted by the public; so much so that victim compliance is sometimes viewed as part of the victim role. In an article written about Bernhard Goetz, who shot four youths who allegedly attempted to rob him in a subway, Smith suggested that New Yorkers have accepted street crime as a fact of life.

> Parents in the most fashionable part of New York, the Upper East Side, were instructing their children to hand over their bus pass or their lunch money to teenage muggers who prowled the streets like leopards looking for tender gazelles. It was streetwise to hand over the money quickly, lest one be knifed. People otherwise very active in their lives trained themselves to be passive on the streets. (Smith, 1985: 63)

More recent research suggests there is an alternative to resistance or compliance. In their study of stranger victimizations, Block and Skogan (1984) distinguished between no resistance, forceful resistance and nonforceful resistance. Forceful resistance occurs where the victim used weapons, hit, scratched, or otherwise physically resisted the offender. Nonforceful resistance involved arguing or reasoning with the offender, yelling or screaming to attract the attention of others or to scare the offender away. Nonforceful resistance was associated with attack by the offender only slightly more often than no resistance at all.

Block and Skogan (1984) caution that their research was a preliminary inquiry and suggest that the source of the data, National Crime Surveys, does not provide information on the sequencing of actions in a violent attack. Hence, it is unknown under what conditions nonforceful resistance is a useful option for victims. In other words, the prevailing wisdom with respect to resistance is that when "any potentially deadly weapon is involved, the correct answer to the implicit demand, your money or your life, is to provide the money" (Zimring and Zuehl, 1986: 30).

As noted earlier, it is not known the extent to which murders are planned as part of the robbery and to what extent they emerge during a robbery encounter. It is known that there are robbery murders that have no apparent indication of victim resistance. It is also known that victim resistance, particularly of a forceful nature, is likely to result in victim injury or death. Neither of the preceding, however, provides direct evidence as to how murders develop in the course of robberies.

The position taken here is that there is not sufficient evidence to negate the view that murders evolve out of the interaction of a robbery encounter. It appears there is substantial indirect evidence to support it.

First, there is evidence to suggest that planning of robberies is not a very elaborate procedure. It is done by a group assembled for this purpose in which the use of the threat of violence by some member of the group is clear. Indeed, the person was chosen for this purpose. Even under the latter conditions, there are members of the robbery group who are concerned with managing the extent of violence expressed by this person, as Walsh (1986) has suggested. Moreover, the primary purpose of this group is the acquisition of money, not the perpetration of violence.

The latter does not address the issue completely. Two or three persons who gather to plan a robbery share a great many values that do not enter into their planning activities. For example, they obviously share a belief that stealing another person's property by force is an acceptable way to acquire money. It is also possible that attitudes about the expression of violence are shared in an unspoken way. At least in current popular accounts, the infliction of violence may be taken as part of the robbery encounter (Cronin and Ludtke, 1989). Injury or murder may be inflicted on the victim, not because the offenders are interested in avoiding later identification, but because it is a shared value of the group. While not being planned for, it is an element that is brought to the encounter.

Second, there are large percentages of offenders who use alcohol or drugs during the perpetration of a robbery. Given the negative effect on judgment of alcohol and drugs, it is more likely that injury and murder would emerge in the encounter accidentally than because they were planned.

Third, because robbery encounters are based on forced compliance rather than consensus, there is a high probability that the encounter will break down because of unanticipated features. A police car may drive by unexpectedly and observe the robbery. A woman in the setting may panic and start screaming uncontrollably. Some male in the setting may decide to play the role of "hero" and attack the offender. Given the nervousness and anxiety of offenders in this setting, any one or all of these may trigger fatal violence.

Finally, given the tenuous and unstable sociological nature of robbery encounters, it is highly probable that a breakdown in communication can occur. Aside from the obvious forms of resistance by the victim, there is behavior that could be interpreted by the offenders as an effort to delay or "stall" the offender. The fatal consequences of such a perceived effort by the victim are given below.

John Jones, a 47-year-old-black man was a customer in a grocery store when two gunmen entered it and robbed it. When Jones did not respond quickly enough to an order by the gunmen he was shot once. He later died from the gunshot wound in the chest. The offenders were arrested on information supplied by a police informant who was told of the incident by the offenders. During the lineup the witnesses could not positively identify the offenders, so the prosecutor refused to prosecute.

CONFRONTATIONAL VIOLENCE: ASSAULTS AND MURDERS

Strangers injure and murder one another in settings that do not involve robberies. They interact with each other spontaneously in unserious settings such as bars, lounges, and parties. In a small number of encounters, a conflict occurs between the two interactants; in even smaller numbers, these conflicts escalate to a violent exchange and, on occasion, murder.

While inconsequentiality is a characteristic of unserious settings, the rules and topics of interaction in such settings are not guaranteed. "Safe" topics of conversations tend to be trivial or commonplace. Opening conversational gambits include comments on the weather, the drinks, sporting events, or the decor of the bar. Aside from these topics, the wide variety of strangers that a person can interact with opens the possibility that almost anything one says or does can be misunderstood or regarded as an insult by another.

The range of possibilities is illustrated by the results of a study by Simmons. He asked his respondents to list those things or persons they regarded as deviant.

It was an interesting question because, even after a great deal of grouping and combining, the 180 subjects had called no less than two hundred and fifty-two distinct acts and persons deviant. The sheer range of responses predictably included homosexuals, prostitutes, drug addicts, radicals, and criminals. But it also included liars, career women, Democrats, reckless drivers, atheists, Christians, suburbanites, the retired, young folks, card players, bearded men, artists, pacifists, priests, prudes, hippies, straights, girls who wear makeup, the President, conservatives, integrationists, executives, divorcees, perverts, motorcycle gangs, smart-alec students, know-it-all professors, modern people, and Americans. (Simmons, 1969: 3)

It is worth noting that persons who have to interact regularly with strangers in unserious settings, such as bartenders, develop a repertoire of responses and rules for interaction that avoid disagreement and insult. Topics on which a bartender might find himself or herself in disagreement with others tend to be responded to with a minimal nod of assent or a noncommittal response. Some people who work in these settings rule out discussion of topics like religion or politics to prevent any confrontations.

Not surprisingly, one of the characteristics that distinguishes confrontational violence between strangers from similar violence between people known to one another is the trivial nature of the event that caused the confrontation. Not only is it not surprising because of the nature of the setting, it is not surprising because stranger offenders and victims share no previous history. Athens gives an example of how trivial events lead to murder:

I was sitting at a bar drinking a beer when this guy sitting next to me went to play the pinball machine. When he came back to the bar, he said, "You've been drinking my beer. I had a full can of beer when I went over to play that pinball machine." He said, "You better buy me another can of beer." I said, "Shit no, I ain't." At first I didn't know whether he really thought I had drank some of his beer or was just trying to bluff me into buying him a can, but when he later said, "You're gonna buy me another fucking can of beer," I knew then he was handing me that to start some crap so I knew for sure that I wasn't gonna buy him any beer. He told me again to buy him a beer. I said, "Hell, no." I figured if I showed him that I wasn't gonna buy him a beer he wouldn't push it, but he said, "You better go on and buy me another fucking beer." All I said then was, "I don't want any trouble; I'm just out of the pen, so go on and leave me alone cause I ain't about to buy you any beer." He just kept looking. Then I started thinking he was out to do something to me. He pulled out a knife and made for me, and I shot him once in the arm. He kept on coming so I had to finish him off. He was out to kill me. (Athens, 1980: 21)

Opening Moves

Those who have considered the interactional sequence leading to confrontational violence among strangers and nonstrangers suggest that one way a violent encounter begins is with an identity attack (Luckenbill, 1977; Felson, 1978). Such an attack can consist of an insult, verbal comments that disparage another's character, or an action that is perceived as intentional and negative by another. In evaluating his processural theory, Felson (1984) has suggested that while it explains retaliatory violence, it does not explain the initial attack. Limiting the discussion to bars, there are several variables that contribute to the initial attack.

First, it was noted in earlier chapters that bars vary in their decorum, kinds of customers, and behavioral expectations. Graham, La Rocque, Yetman, Ross and Guistra (1980) studied aggression in Vancouver bars. One of the strongest explanatory factors was the barroom environment. The bars with the highest amount of aggression were characterized by loud and abusive language, lack of cleanliness, inexpensive physical surroundings, high percentages of American Indians and unkempt patrons, patrons drinking rapidly and becoming highly intoxicated, a downtown location, tables crowded together, and unfriendly barworkers. This factor was strongly related (r = .59) to both physical and nonphysical aggression.

Second, age is an important variable in explaining aggression in bars. Felson, Baccaglini, and Gmelch (1986) studied bars in Ireland and Albany, New York and concluded:

> The best predictor of aggression in these data was age. Bars that served youthful patrons were much more likely to experience incidents of verbal and physical aggression, and verbal incidents

involving youthful patrons were more likely to be become physically violent. Thus, it appears that one of the reasons aggression occurs in bars is that they are places where young adults congregate and come into contact. However, participants in aggressive incidents were no younger than the general clientele. The finding (in the American sample) that the age of a bar's clientele predicted the frequency of aggression in that bar, but that the participants in aggressive incidents were no younger than the general clientele, suggests a contextual effect: youths are more likely to fight when they are with other youth than when they are among older persons.
(Felson, Baccaglini and Gmelch, 1986: 163-164)

As the authors note, the finding of homogeneity in ages in the bar's clientele suggests that audiences or third parties may play a role in instigating and supporting violence in this setting.

Third, there is the contribution of alcohol to the instigation of violence. Gibbs has pointed out that the consumption of alcohol affects primary and 'secondary cognitive appraisal. "'Primary appraisal' refers to the person's evaluation of the situation in terms of his well-being, and 'secondary appraisal' refers to the person's assessment of the coping resources available to deal with the situation." (Gibbs, 1986: 139)

The consumption of alcohol can lead a person to perceive a less than complete representation of his environment. When a person's perceptual field is narrowed, random fluctuations in the environment can mean drastic changes in his or her perception of the setting. Actions by others may appear arbitrary and inconsistent to the perceiver because he or she has an overly simplified view of the setting. Thus, intoxicated people may be very insulted by a statement or action that others view as trivial.

Gibbs suggested that the perceptual simplification and reduction of attention to outside cues have another consequence. Because of the fewer number of cues perceived, cognized and mentally processed, there may be a greater sense of power or mastery of the setting which translates into behavior.

A man of power has certain rights, privileges, duties and obligations. Events that seem inconsequential to others may require a response from the powerful. A breach of drinking-protocol at the far end of the bar may be an irritant to the average man, but it flies in the face of the powerful man's authority. After all, it is his duty to maintain protocol in his bar-territory. (Gibbs, 1986: 143)

The latter view is not inconsistent with Felson's (1984) belief that aggression is a form of social control. It is, in his view, a self-help approach in which the offender punishes the victim for what he or she considers a violation of norms or orders. In other words, violence toward a victim may be punishment for what he or she has done or will fail to do.

The type of setting, age of the clientele, amount of intoxication, and feeling that someone deserves punishment are given as instigating features in bar violence for strangers and nonstrangers. However, given the wide variety of strangers that go to bars and the different kinds of behaviors to which they can take exception, it would be expected that the source and content of disputes between strangers will show more variation than nonstrangers. Indeed, given the possible reasons suggested by Simmons (1969) in the previous section and the instigating factors listed above, it is reasonable to suggest that the number of disputes initiated by strangers, other things being equal, may be more numerous than those involving nonstrangers. While strangers may initiate more disputes for more different reasons, proportionately fewer stranger disputes may escalate to physical violence, as research in a later section will suggest.

Evaluation, Response, and the Role of Audiences

Luckenbill (1977) identified five additional stages beyond the initial attack in the interactional patterns of homicide. These include (1) an evaluation by the offender that the initial attack is personally offensive; (2) a retaliation in the form of verbal or physical attack; (3) the victim refuses to alter his or her insulting behavior or physically retaliates; (4) a commitment by the two participants to resolve their differences by violence; (5) the aftermath.

Felson and Steadman's (1983) research on situational aspects of assaults and non-felony homicides supports the Luckenbill theory and their own formulation of the "impression management" of violence. The first of their three stages involves identity attacks where attempts to influence the antagonist fail. The second stage involves threats and evasive action while the third stage involves physical attack (Felson, 1978).

If what Luckenbill, Felson, and Felson and Steadman describe as the general interactional process describes encounters resulting in homicides, how do fatal encounters between strangers differ? A major difference occurs in the evaluation of the meaning of the opening attack. Is the insult by the victim to be construed as an insult or a careless or accidental remark made by someone who is drunk, crazy, or simply joking? There are two general answers to the question.

First, based on the victim's past behavior, the offender will make an inference whether the insulting behavior was intentional. Given that nonstranger violence is characterized by a previous relationship, there may have been frequent "rehearsals" of the confrontation that leads to violence in an unserious setting. For example, Luckenbill (1977) cites the case of the woman who told her boyfriend that she had been seeing other men and that they "pleased her more than the offender." While such a statement may be construed by the offender as offensive, it is when the conflict is played out again in the public setting that violence may result. Thus, if the woman in the preceding instance flirts with others in a bar, because of past experiences, the boyfriend interprets her behavior as an insulting gesture.

Second, an important factor in evaluating the remarks of another is the interpretation placed on the behavior in question by third parties or audiences. If a person is speaking to a friend or acquaintance, he or she knows what kinds of topics can be broached in unserious settings, which topics can be joked about, and what cannot. Where the interactants are strangers, the interpretation placed on the interaction by third parties becomes disproportionately important.

Both Felson and Luckenbill have incorporated the role of audiences in their conceptualization of violent interaction. For example, in stage 2, Luckenbill found that the offender learned the meaning of the victim's move from inquiries of or statements from bystanders in 21 percent of the homicide cases. The following case illustrates the point.

The offender and his friend were sitting in a booth at a tavern drinking beer. The offender's friend told him that the offender's girlfriend was "playing" with another man (victim) at the other end of the bar. The offender looked at them and asked his friend if he thought something was going on. The friend responded, "I wouldn't let that guy fool around with [her] if she was mine." The offender agreed, and suggested to his friend that his girlfriend and the victim be shot for their actions. His friend said that only the victim should be shot, not the girlfriend. (Luckenbill, 1977: 181)

A study by Zahn and Sagi (1987) provides information on the role of audiences in stranger homicides. For homicide data in nine cities, Zahn and Sagi (1987) divided the stranger category into those associated with and without felonies. As expected, most of the stranger felony categories involved robberies.   An example of stranger non-felony homicides is given below:

> A thirty-one year old black female parked her car in a driveway for a short time in a heavy snow.   The car got stuck.   When she returned, the offender's father yelled at her and hit her child.   The offender, a twenty-year-old black male, came out of the house, shot and killed the victim, and wounded her two children. (Zahn and Sagi, 1987: 382)

Zahn and Sagi reported a surprising 89 percent of stranger non-felony offenses were witnessed by at least one other person. Unfortunately, the authors did not examine the relationship between audiences and confrontational stranger homicide in each of the nine cities.

There is very little known about the effect of audiences on non-fatal forms of stranger violence.   However, given the close relationship between assaults and homicide mentioned in earlier chapters, it is reasonable to suppose that audiences may play a very important role in other forms of confrontational stranger violence.

Beyond their mere presence, audiences do seem to increase the amount of violence by instigation or encouragement of the principal actor. To determine the effect of third parties, Felson (1982) interviewed a sample of ex-mental patients, ex-criminal offenders, and a carefully selected representative sample of the general population.   They were asked to describe in detail four incidents varying in severity.   The first task was to "recall the last dispute that you can remember clearly that you were involved, where a gun or knife was drawn or used."

The second incident involved describing an incident in which only hitting or slapping was involved.   The third incident that the subjects were asked to describe was one in which there was a bad argument with screaming, shouting, and name-calling, but no physical violence.   The fourth incident to be described was one in which the subject was very angry with someone else, but said nothing about it.   For each incident, subjects were asked to describe in sequence the actions of each participant.

Felson found that the presence of third parties increased the severity of the incident when males were involved, but not females.   When the effect of third party instigation of a conflict was examined, Felson found that instigation increased the odds of a verbal and hitting/slapping dispute. There was less instigation in disputes involving weapons, apparently because with the presence of weapons, third parties were less likely to want to encourage the conflict or feel the need to do so.

Felson and Steadman (1983) and Felson, Ribner, and Siegel (1984) examined the effects of third parties in greater detail. Felson, et al. (1984) found that third parties engaged in verbal or physical aggression in 59 percent of the incidents studied. There was no difference between assault and homicide offenses.

Major participants were more violent if their significant others were also aggressive. In other words, offenders struck more blows and victims engaged in more physical attacks when their friends and relatives were aggressive.

Third parties are more supportive of violence involving younger offenders. In other words, not only are young males more likely to engage in violence, they are more likely to do so when other young males are present and support violence. They do this either because third parties, by their own aggression, define the setting as appropriate for violence or because third parties function as audiences for whom victims and offenders are managing impressions (Felson, et al., 1984).

For homicide or murder, there are other differences between exploitative and confrontational violence among strangers. Zahn and Sagi (1987) found that in exploitative violence such as stranger robbery homicides, the interracial component involves black offenders and white victims. While white offenders tended to rob and kill white victims (65.5%), black offenders tended to victimize white victims (61.2%). For confrontational homicides, 21 percent of the victims and offenders were of different races.

Offenders seek targets with something valuable to rob; these settings are also often populated by older people who have responsibilities as owners, managers, or employees. Thus, it is not surprising that stranger felony homicides involve a much larger difference in the ages of victims and offenders than other victim/offender combinations. For the stranger felony homicides studied by Zahn and Sagi (1987), the mean age of victims was 40 years while the mean age of offenders was 26 years, a difference of 14 years. The difference in years for stranger non-felony homicides was one; the mean age of victims was 30 years while the mean age for offenders was 29. All other combinations of victim/offender relationships differed by no more than two years.

Zahn and Sagi (1987) found that the percent of stranger interracial homicides was much lower for confrontational violence in comparison with exploitative violence. Within the category of confrontational violence, strangers are more often involved in interracial murders. Przybylski (1987) examined the association between victim/offender relationships and a number of possible etiological variables using information on 4,123 assault homicides between 1976-1983 in the six Illinois counties that make up the Chicago Standard Metropolitan Statistical Area. Of the 3,054 intraracial murders, 12 percent involved strangers. Of the 195 interracial murders, 36 percent involved strangers.

As indicated previously, it is not surprising that stranger robbery murders or homicides involve black offenders and white victims. As other writers have noted, social and economic inequities play an important role in choice of target. (Block, 1977; Cook, 1976). White victims more often possess money or property that is coveted by black offenders. Some of these encounters culminate in murder.

In confrontational murders between strangers, however, the interracial component takes on a different form. When Przybylski examined the interracial combinations, he found that white offenders killed black victims somewhat more often than black offenders killed white victims (38.4% vs. 31.6%). The more equitable distribution of racial combinations of victims and offenders in stranger assault murders is consistent with the view that confrontational murder is precipitated by insults, arguments, fights, and brawls that can be participated in by both black and white offenders. The next section will offer an explanation of why confrontational murders among strangers, in comparison with nonstrangers, are more frequently interracial.

Stopping It: Bartenders, Accounts, and Audiences

The view of confrontational violence that has been presented is one in which, beginning with an identity attack that consists of an insult or argument, interaction between victim and offender escalates through a series of threats and counter-threats to a fatal outcome (Luckenbill, 1977). Because there are many more confrontations that end with little or no violence than confrontations with fatal outcomes, it is important to consider how possibly fatal confrontations are diverted to less violent ends.

In the case of the bar as an unserious setting, it appears that the bartender is an important figure in beginning and ending violent confrontations. It is true that the inconsequential nature of behavior in a bar makes a wide variety of behavior possible. The possible limits of behavior are likely to be extended even further when there are strangers in the setting.

But no matter how flexible the boundaries of a bar may be, they do exist, and the person in charge of maintaining them is often the bartender. Hence, it is no surprise that the most frequent cause of physical and verbal disputes is the bartender's refusal to serve a customer. For example, in the Albany bars studied by Felson, et al. (1986), 22.8 percent of the verbal disputes and 24.1 percent of the physical disputes involved a refusal to serve.

Bouncers---persons employed to eject disorderly customers---were most often present in the bars studied by Felson, et al. (1986), when there were many young patrons. While the authors were not able to specify a relationship between the use of bouncers and aggression, their analysis does suggest that the "use of bouncers most likely reduces the frequency of aggression." (Felson, et al., 1986: 160)

While bars are tolerant of a variety of deviant behavior, most set limits at the expression of violence. This is especially true for after-hours bars where police and other officials have been paid to ignore their existence.

They come here to have a ball, so you go along with them. That's what the place is---for people to have a good time. They feel a little freer here than in a public bar. After all, they're with their own kind, and they don't have to be on guard all the time because they know they're in good hands with us---like Allstate. So they're going to drink more here and really get it on with the broads. If it's for fun, fine, but when they get mad and take each other seriously, we have to step in and cool it off. We can't have a couple of gorillas tearing up property and blocking other people's acts. (Roebuck and Frese, 1976: 128)

Bartenders are responsible for intervening in conflicts between customers to prevent their escalation. Usually, a request that the customer cease his or her annoying behavior and leave is sufficient to prevent any further difficulties. Sometimes, however, the bartender is the victim of his or her own intervention.

Emile Garcia was working as a bartender when Mark Solliday entered the bar, sat next to a female patron, and began saying annoying things to her. Garcia advised Solliday that he would not be served, and asked him to leave. Solliday left, and returned about an hour later with a gun. He fired a shot into the ceiling, and Garcia began to walk toward him. Solliday then fired several shots at Garcia. Garcia grabbed Solliday and both men fell to the floor. It was noted that Garcia had suffered a bullet wound of the abdomen. Police responded, and Solliday was taken into custody at the scene. Garcia was transported to the hospital, where he received treatment until he died two days later.

Felson (1978) has suggested that the escalation of a violent encounter may be prevented by the interactants when one or the other gives "accounts." In other words, if an individual offers an explanation of his behavior to another that makes it appear justifiable to the latter, the possibility of a violent conclusion is reduced. This can take the form of assuring the other person that the insult was not intended or that his or her dispute was for specific justifiable reasons. Such a giving of an account can occur before the perceived attack on the other, immediately after, or after the victim of his or her attack reproaches the offender and asks for an explanation (Felson, 1984).

Besides instigating and supporting violence in unserious settings, third parties can act to mediate the conflict, although this hypothesis is not clearly supported. In examining 70 incidents of felonious assault, manslaughter or murder, Felson, et al. (1984) found that mediation by third parties occurred in 12.9 percent of the cases. However, instigation, identity, and physical attacks account for between 17.1 percent and 20.0 percent of the behavior of third parties. In a more complex analysis, when third parties mediate, offenders deliver fewer blows. Mediation was not significantly related to physical attacks by the victim (Felson, et al., 1984). While third parties do mediate and thereby reduce the severity of violent encounters, more often they encourage them.

In one of the few considerations of the role of strangers in bar violence, Graham, et al. (1980) found that bars could be classified as to whether they were open and friendly to strangers or closed where the inhabitants of the bar kept to themselves and talked only with members of their own group. She found that the variable of openness to strangers was significantly related to nonphysical aggression in the bar (r = .19), but not physical aggression (r = .09).

The latter is consistent with the view that strangers may take exception to and be insulted by a greater variety of topics than nonstrangers. What the Graham, et al. (1980) finding suggests is that fewer of these disputes escalate to physical violence. What accounts for this?

A major reason may be that the stranger, even with one or two friends, simply finds himself or herself outnumbered. The interactional nature of a bar is established by its regular clientele. Unless the dispute is with someone who is equally unknown in the bar, the stranger who initiates a conflict may find that the audience and the bartender is solidly on the side of his or her opponent. In these circumstances, the stranger is likely not to want to escalate the conflict.

Such is not always the case. There are occasions where audiences may want to promote a violent encounter, particularly where they have a general basis for their dislike of the stranger. Where strangers of different races interact in a bar, given the amount of ignorance, mutual prejudice and racism that exists, there is ample opportunity for misunderstanding. Where one of the interactants is of the same race as the bartender and the audience, and the other is not, the probability of an escalation to a violent, and possibly fatal, encounter is heightened. The latter provides a possible explanation for Pyzybylski's finding that stranger assault murders were more frequently interracial than nonstranger murders.

There are, of course, no guarantees that a violent escalation can be prevented. A bartender may order the persons involved in the conflict to leave the setting. While that may resolve the immediate problem, it may mean that the conflict is transferred to another setting.

The incident was recorded by the police to have occurred at 12:20 in the morning in a neighborhood tavern. Two men, who were regular customers, got into an argument and fight with four customers who were unknown to those present. The owner of the tavern told the four customers to leave and they did so. Later, as one of the regular customers was leaving he was shot to death by one of the four who had returned.

Finally, a major question is the extent to which a member of an audience risks becoming a victim in any effort to intervene. A study by Wallace (1964) of 574 victims of violence in San Juan indicated that one-fifth of the cases involved an audience; half of the audience members were injured as a result of their participation. What evidence there is suggests that intervention in a violent confrontation carries considerable risks of injury to the intervening party.

NOTES

1. Muggings refer to "acts of robbery committed in public or
    semipublic places, usually by young and unskilled predators."
    (Lejeune, 1977: 123)

2. John Lofland notes the research of Hebb and Thompson (1968)
    which concludes that there is a strong positive relation between
    position on the phylogenetic scale and capacity for rage, violative
    reactivity, and disorganized behavior. Hebb suggest that this
    relation is a consequence of the complexity of the nervous system.
    The most complex neural systems are those capable of the strongest
    responses. "As the creature with the most complex neural system
    yet to evolve, man may also be the most threatenable." (Lofland,
    1968: 43)

REFERENCES

Athens, L. H. (1980). Violent criminal acts and actors. Boston: Routledge & Kegan Paul.

Block, R. (1977). Violent crime: Environment, interaction, and death. Lexington: Lexington Books.

Block, R., & Skogan, W. G. (1984). The dynamics of violence between strangers: Victim resistance and outcomes in rape, assault, and robbery. Evanston, Illinois: Center for Urban Affairs and Policy Research.

Cook, P. J. (1980). Reducing injury and death rates in robbery. Policy Analysis, 6, 21-45.

Cook, P. J. (1982). The role of firearms in violent crime. In M. E. Wolfgang and N. A. Weiner (Eds.), Criminal violence (pp. 236-291). Beverly Hills: Sage Publications.

Cook, P. J. (1976). A strategic choice analysis of robbery. In W. G. Skogan (Ed.), Sample surveys of the victims of crime (pp. 173-187). Cambridge: Ballinger Publishing Co.

Cronin, M., & Ludtke, M. (1989). Wilding in the night. Time Magazine, 133, 20-21.

Einstadter, W. J. (1969). The social organization of armed robbery. Social Problems, 17, 64-83.

Felson, R. B. (1978). Aggression as impression management. Social Psychology, 41, 205-213.

Felson, R. B. (1982). Impression management and the escalation of aggression and violence. Social Psychology Quarterly, 45, 245-254.

Felson, R. B. (1984). Patterns of aggressive social interaction. In A. Mummendey (Ed.), Social psychology of aggression: From individual behavior to social interaction (pp. 107-126). Berlin: Springer-Verlag.

Felson, R. B., Baccaglini, W., & Gmelch, G. (1986). Bar-room brawls: Aggression and violence in Irish and American bars. In A. Campbell and J. J. Gibbs (Eds.), Violent transactions: The limits of personality. (pp. 153-166). Oxford: Basil Blackwell.

Felson, R. B., Ribner, S. A., & Siegel, M. S. (1984). Age and the effect of third parties during criminal violence. Sociology and Social Research, 68, 452-462.

Felson, R. B., & Steadman, H. J. (1983). Situational factors in disputes leading to criminal violence. Criminology: An Interdisciplinary Journal, 21, 59-74.

Gibbs, J. J. (1986). Alcohol consumption, cognition, and context: Examining tavern violence. In A. Campbell and J. J. Gibbs (Eds.), Violent transactions: The limits of personality. (pp. 133-151). Oxford: Basil Blackwell.

Graham, K., La Rocque, L., Yetman, R., Ross, T. J., & Guistra, E. (1980). Aggression and barroom environments. Journal of Studies on Alcohol, 41, 277-292.

Hindelang, M. J., Gottfredson, M. R., & Garofalo, J. (1978). Victims of personal crimes: An empirical foundation for a theory of personal victimization. Cambridge: Ballinger Publishing Co.

Katz, J. Seductions of crime. New York: Basic Books, Inc.

Lejeune, R. (1977). The management of a mugging. Urban Life and Culture, 6, 123-148.

Lejeune, R., & Alex, N. (1973). On being mugged: The event and its aftermath. Urban Life and Culture, 2, 259-287.

Letkeman, P. (1973). Crime as work. Englewood Cliffs: Prentice-Hall.

Lorenz Dietz, M. (1983). Killing for profit. Chicago: Nelson-Hall.

Luckenbill, D. F. (1980). Patterns of force in robbery. Deviant Behavior, 1, 361-378.

Luckenbill, D. F. (1981). Generating compliance. Urban Life, 10, 25-46.

Luckenbill, D. F. (1977). Criminal homicide as a situated transaction. Social Problems, 25, 176-186.

Przybylski, R. (1987). Stranger murder in the Chicago metropolitan area: An analysis of the Victim-Level Murder file. Masters Thesis: Southern Illinois University.

Roebuck, J. B., & Frese, W. (1976). The Rendezvous: A case study of an after-hours club. New York: Free Press.

Simmons, J. L. (1969). Deviants. Glendessary Press.

Smith, A. (1985). The city as the OK corral. Esquire, 62-64.

Wallace, S. E. (1965). Patterns of violence in San Juan. In W. C. Reckless and C. L. Newman (Eds.), Interdisciplinary problems in criminology: Papers of the American Society of Criminology (pp. 43-48). Columbus, Ohio: American Society of Criminology.

Walsh, D. (1986). Heavy business: Commercial burglary and robbery. London: Routledge & Kegan Paul.

Zahn, M. A., & Sagi, P. C. (1987). Stranger homicides in nine American cities. Journal of Criminal Law and Criminology, 78, 377-397.

Zimring, F. E. & Zuehl, J. (1986). Victim injury and death in urban robbery: A Chicago study. Journal of Legal Studies, 15, 1-40.

CHAPTER 7

THE SOCIAL RESPONSE TO
STRANGER VIOLENCE

The theoretical perspective that has been described in the preceding chapters has only briefly touched on criminal justice concerns. In describing stranger relationships, the settings in which they typically function, and how those settings can be used for violent purposes, there has been little mention of how law enforcement, courts, and corrections respond to stranger violence. The final chapter examines these issues.

In describing the reaction of the criminal justice system to criminal violence, Black's (1976) theory on the sociology of law is used. In relating the perspective described here to Black's theory, it is necessary to take into account that we are comparing a microsociological theory to a macrosociological one. James Short distinguishes the two levels of explanation.

My use of the term [micro-level] is to distinguish the outcomes of ongoing processes of interaction among actors from those related to the characteristics of social systems and culture. The latter are structural and cultural in nature; the micro-level, by way of contrast, focuses on events and interaction with systems, structures and cultures. (Short, 1985: 54-55)

The theoretical description of stranger relationships and violence described here is of the micro-level variety while Black's theory is treated as a macro-level of explanation. In assessing the implications of the theory given in the preceding chapters to the behavior of law, the intent is not to create a multi-level theory. Rather, the approach taken assumes

177

that a micro-level explanation can raise important questions and useful hypotheses when examined in the context of macro-level theory.

STRANGER VIOLENCE AND THE BEHAVIOR OF LAW

Black (1976) was primarily concerned with showing the relation of law to other social dimensions such as stratification, social structure and organization, culture and social control. Not only are the latter variable aspects of social life, but law is also a quantitative variable.

More generally, the quantity of law is known by the number and scope of prohibitions, obligations, and other standards to which people are subject, and by the rate of legislation, litigation, and adjudication. As a quantitative variable, law is all this and more. (Black, 1976: 3)

Black provided a large number of propositions to show how the quantity of law is related to other social dimensions. For example, <u>law varies inversely with other forms of social control</u> (p. 6). Where other and informal forms of social control exist, law is not active. Where these other forms do not exist, law is very active. Thus, as Chapter 3 indicated, respondents on the National Crime Survey are more likely to report stranger victimizations than those involving family members and friends. What this suggests is that victims often regard their conflicts with family and friends, including violent ones, as matters that can be resolved without law. On the other hand, law is needed to resolve conflict with strangers largely because urban victims have no other recourse than to call the police.

Gottfredson and Hindelang (1979a, 1979b) have argued that the quantity of law is explained by the gravity of the infraction against legal norms rather than the social dimensions described by Black. It is the seriousness of the offense, "the extent of harm suffered [by the victim that] is the principle determinant of the quantity of law" (Gottfredson and Hindelang, 1979a: 5). After an extensive analysis of National Crime Survey results for 1974, 1975, and 1976, the authors could find little to support Black's propositions. The authors did find, however, that stranger victimization was slightly better reported than nonstranger victimization, which is consistent with Black's assertion. However, given the difficulties in recording nonstranger violence described in Chapter 3, it is difficult to judge how well NCS results can be used to test hypotheses about stranger-nonstranger involvement in crime.

Some additional support for Black's theory is available from considering the results in Chapter 2. There it was pointed out that stranger homicides were consistently underreported at the national level in comparison with other victim/offender relationships. If seriousness is the most important determinant of the quantity of law, then it should follow that stranger homicides would be the best reported, given that they are more serious than other forms of homicides. On the other hand, if the reporting of stranger homicides is determined by factors other than, or in addition to, seriousness, the result documented in Chapter 2 should prevail.[1]

It seems likely that seriousness is only one of several dimensions that determine how decisions are made in criminal justice. In a review of aspects that enter into criminal justice decision making, Gottfredson and Gottfredson state that "from the host of offender, victim, decision-maker and situational facts that potentially influence individual decision making, three appear to play a persistent and major role throughout the system: the seriousness of the offense, the prior criminal conduct of the offender, and the personal relationship between the victim of the crime and the offender" (Gottfredson and Gottfredson, 1988: 257-258).

Finally, it is a misunderstanding of Black's theory to believe that the quantity of law can be encapsulated in a variable of seriousness. In Black's view, seriousness is one object of explanation by a theory of law. A major aim of a theory of law is:

> to predict and explain variation in the quantity of law with its location and direction in social space, defined by the characteristics of the people involved, their relationships with each other, and the larger social context in which they interact. It should be noted that from this standpoint the nature of "crime" and its "seriousness" are expressions of law itself, since law defines the conduct to be known as "crime" and the degree to which it is to be handled as "serious."
> (Black, 1976: 19)

Macro- and Micro-Level Explanations of Strangers

One way to conceive of relationships is that "people vary in the degree to which they participate in one another's lives." (Black, 1976: 40) The resulting degree of intimacy or relational distance varies from the most intimate relationships to none at all. At one end of the continuum are the intimate relationships of spouses and families where there is extensive and intensive mutual participation in each other's lives. The relational distance becomes greater as friends and acquaintances are considered and is greatest with stranger relationships. The latter are decidedly distinct from instances where there is no relationship at all.[2]

In defining stranger relationships, Black (1976) and Lofland (1973) both assume that a characteristic of stranger relationships is minimal contact between people. However, this assumption has very different consequences for the two theorists. For Black, the minimal nature of the contact was a quantity, a point on the continuum of a relational distance variable. The relevant problem then becomes stating the propositional relationship between relational distance and the quantity of law. Because there are propositions about the quantity of law and other social dimensions, it becomes possible to link the behavior of law, relational distance, and major aspects of society.

For Lofland, the minimal nature of contacts between strangers was a quality. These minimal contacts meant that little was known about strangers except their categorical characteristics and where they were observed. The major problem for Lofland was trying to explain how, given the nature of cities and the omnipresence of strangers, it was possible to interact with strangers so as to carry on routine urban activities.

The two perspectives do not conflict, they simply employ a micro-level and a macro-level of explanation; they are more likely to talk past each other than to each other (Short, 1985). Consider, for example, the following proposition: the relationship between law and relational distance is curvilinear (Black, 1976: 41). In other words, law is used infrequently in a violent conflict between intimates and when we have no contact with others. The quantity of law reaches a maximum when the relational distance refers to strangers.

Black's proposition focuses on how and when law is used with different relationships among people. It does not follow that nonlegal or informal sanctions are unimportant as the preceding proposition on social control indicated. Rather, it is a question of relative proportions: when is law used more often than other sanctions?

However, to ignore consideration of informal sanctions and the wide variety of interaction that occurs among strangers is to lose sight of the vast amount of social behavior that is only remotely related to the behavior of law. For example, a stranger may enter a bar, order a drink, and refuse to speak to anyone, even when others make opening remarks. His or her cold refusal to respond may be because of a large number of reasons that have little to do with law. Others may interpret his or her silence as rudeness, but hardly a matter of law. If an explanation of stranger violence assumes that violent outcomes result from routine settings and encounters among strangers, then Black has little to contribute toward understanding those routine stranger relationships.

On the other hand, when strangers exhibit behavior that is relevant to law, Black's propositions offer a rich and interesting set of possibilities. The following section will explore how the quantity of law is related to stranger violence.

The Quantity of Law and Stranger Violence

The research does seem to support the view that the quantity of law reaches a maximum when strangers are involved in violence. Several studies reported in chapter 3 indicate that stranger violence is reported more often to the police than violence involving nonstrangers. The greater quantity of law for stranger offenders is also evident in Lundsgaarde's (1977) study of Houston homicide. He found that while over 90 percent of the reported homicides resulted in the apprehension of an offender, fewer than 50 percent of the offenders were negatively sanctioned.

Much of the difference could be accounted for by examining victim/offender relationships. Over 40 percent of the homicides involving family members and relatives and more than 35 percent of homicides involving friends and associates were "no billed" by the grand jury, no charge was filed, or a charge of "nolle prosequi" was entered. For homicides involving strangers, only 24 percent were so processed. As a result, a much higher proportion of nonstranger homicide offenders as compared to stranger offenders were diverted out of the criminal justice system at the early stages.

Stranger homicide offenders were also given harsher dispositions when compared to other types of victim/offender relationships. They received a mean prison term of 27.9 years, while domestic homicides, and friend and associate homicides had means of 7.6 and 10.1 years, respectively. Finally, 9.1 percent of the stranger homicide offenders received the death penalty, while none of the other two victim/offender types received that disposition.

Lundsgaarde (1977) hypothesized that the severity of the penalty for homicides in Houston varies inversely with the intimacy of the relationship. In an analysis of Texas law and its implementation, he found excessive reliance was placed on legal categories such as "malice," "state of mind," "intent," and "motive," the meanings of which were grounded in a custom-laden concept of "the reasonable man." On that basis, if the offender could justify his act to the grand jury as one precipitated by a stimulus from the victim (self-defense), the behavior was downgraded to justifiable homicide or murder without malice. Thus, a man who murdered his wife's lover after catching them in flagrante delicto would be "no billed" and released from police custody.

Homicides involving strangers were another matter. There is the question of unprovoked violence. While violence among intimates might be justified as self-defense, no such rationale is likely to exist for stranger homicides.

A study by the Vera Institute (1977) found that the two most important factors affecting the outcome of felony cases were the victim/offender relationship and the offender's prior criminal history. Felony charges were dismissed more often because of complainant non-cooperation when victims and offenders knew one another than when they were strangers. Among the offenses of rape, assault, robbery and grand larceny, 87 percent involving prior relationships were dismissed. For the same type of felonies involving stranger relationships, only 29 percent were dismissed.

The most dramatic effects of victim/offender relationship were found for robbery cases. Among the 34 robbery arrests involving strangers, 88 percent were convicted of at least one charge; 68 percent were convicted on felony charges. By contrast, among the 19 robbery arrests involving a prior relationship, only 37 percent were convicted of any charges and 5 percent were convicted of a felony charge.

For the same two groups of robbery arrests, 65 percent of the stranger robbery cases were given jail or prison terms, but only 21 percent of the cases involving a prior relationship were given a similar sentence. Thirty-two percent of the stranger robberies were given felony sentences of over one year. None of the robberies involving prior relationships were given felony sentences of more than one year (Vera Institute, 1977).

In a study of the extent to which a wide variety of offenses resulted in conviction, Forst (1981) found that those involving strangers were more likely to result in conviction. For example, in New Orleans, 48 percent of the arrests for all offenses involving strangers resulted in conviction. For friends and acquaintances, and family members, the corresponding conviction rate was 30 percent and 19 percent. In the same city, robberies involving strangers resulted in conviction in 37 percent of the cases. For robberies of family members (7%) and friends and acquaintances (21%), the conviction rate was much lower. Likewise, for other violent offenses, stranger offenders were more frequently convicted (35%) than friends and acquaintances (19%) or family members (16%).

In describing the three important factors in criminal justice decisions (seriousness, prior record, and victim/offender relationship), Gottfredson and Gottfredson summarize the impact of strangers on discretionary decisions.

The major pattern may be stated succinctly: It is preferred that the criminal justice process not deal with criminal acts between nonstrangers. Nearly every decision maker in the process seeks alternatives for criminal acts between relatives, friends, and acquaintances. The gravest dispositions are reserved continuously for events between strangers. Victims report nonstranger events less frequently, police arrest less frequently, prosecutors charge less frequently, and so on through the system. (Gottfredson and Gottfredson, 1988: 259)

CONFRONTATIONAL AND EXPLOITATIVE VIOLENCE AMONG STRANGERS

From Black's theory, one of the reasons that robberies and robbery murders are the more serious offenses is that they involve a greater quantity of law. They involve a greater quantity of law, in turn, because the type of victim or target is one who is more likely to invoke the law. Thus, by definition a robbery victim has property or goods that the offender wants and takes by force. In Black's perspective that would suggest that the victim is of a higher social class or has more wealth than the offender. The quantity of law not only varies directly with the amount of stratification, it also varies directly with rank, which is the location of a person in relation to others.

Law, Black suggests, has direction. It is applied upward or downward in relation to our own rank. It can, of course, be applied to people of our own rank. However, <u>downward law is greater than upward law</u> (p. 21). This means that in a robbery, the victim, who is more wealthy, is more likely to invoke the law against the offender, who is less wealthy.

The vertical direction of law is opposite that of deviant behavior. The downward direction of law is in response to upward deviance and vice versa.

It may be argued that a wealthy victim may more frequently invoke the law against a poor offender, but the converse is not true. A wealthy offender who robs a poor victim may find that the victim is more than willing to invoke any variety of civil and criminal laws available to him or her in the hopes of acquiring some of the offender's wealth. This may be true for victims and offenders who know one another, but not for strangers. In the latter case, it falls upon victims to mobilize severely limited resources in the face of uncertain outcomes.

Unlike robberies and robbery murders, confrontational violence represents a greater predominance of violence among persons of similar rank. Assaults and murders among people of the same rank would involve less law than violence toward someone above our rank and more law than violence toward someone below our rank. This is not to suggest that all confrontational violence is between peers; it is to suggest that, minimally, there is a greater mix of ranks between victims and offenders than is the case in exploitative violence. Because the greater seriousness of robbery is determined by the downward direction of law, it follows that assaults, injuries and murders defined as confrontational violence are less serious.

Within Black's perspective, it can be hypothesized that exploitative stranger violence involves a greater quantity of law than exploitative nonstranger violence. Similarly, confrontational stranger violence has more law than confrontational nonstranger violence. If the quantity of law is maximized in the case of stranger violence then it adds an increment to the quantity of law of the violent act. Hence, robberies involving strangers are treated more seriously than robberies involving nonstrangers. By the same reasoning, confrontational violence among strangers is subject to more law than confrontational violence among nonstrangers. Likewise, exploitative stranger violence is more serious than confrontational stranger violence.

Within the category of confrontational violence, rank is important in explaining the quantity of law. Where there is an economic differential between blacks and whites, there is a difference in ranks. Thus, a violent act by a black man toward a white man involves more law than the reverse. Donald Black cites the research of Johnson (1941) which indicated that blacks who killed whites were treated more severely by the criminal justice system than whites who killed blacks or blacks who killed blacks. Current research on the death penalty shows that black or white offenders who murdered white victims were more frequently given the death penalty. The evidence also shows that blacks who kill whites are given the death penalty more frequently than whites who kill whites, but the important variable is the race of the victim (Acker, 1987).

According to the preceding chapter, exploitative violence more often involves white victims and black offenders. While confrontational stranger violence is also interracial, it more often involves similar proportions of white victims and black offenders. Robberies involve a greater quantity of law because the victim is not only higher in rank, but he or she is white. By contrast, the offender is poorer and black.

The more interesting cases involve racial differentials in confrontational stranger violence. According to Black's theory, blacks who injure or murder whites in unserious settings will be subject to more law than the reverse. Similarly, whites who injure or kill other whites in such settings should be subject to more law than blacks who injure or kill other blacks.

Hypotheses about the violent behavior of strangers can also be derived from social dimensions other than stratification. Organization refers to the corporate aspect of society, the capacity for collective action. Like other dimensions in Black's theory, it is a quantitative variable. Measures of organization "include the presence and number of administrative officers, the centralization and continuity of decision making, and the quantity of collective action itself" (Black, 1976: 85). Because groups can vary in their degree of organization, there is an organizational distance between and among them. Thus, robbery groups are less organized than banks. Further, law is greater in a direction toward less organization than toward more organization (Black, 1976: 92). It follows that the quantity of law is greater in a robbery of a large bank than the robbery of a small store. Where the differences in degree of organization, or organizational distance, is small, the quantity of law is likewise small. Thus, the quantity of law involved in a mugging is less than in a robbery of a store.

Interesting hypotheses are found in looking at the effect of social control and confrontational violence. Respectability refers to the social control to which the individual is subject: the more social control, the less respectability. Where other social controls are weak and law is strong, the more subject the person is to law, the less the respectability. To be subject to criminal law is especially unrespectable.

Because law is greater in a direction toward less respectability than toward more respectability (p. 114), it follows that unrespectable victims involve a smaller quantity of law than respectable victims. Thus, an offender on probation who assaults and injures an ordinary citizen in a bar will be subject to a greater quantity of law than if the victim is also on probation. Likewise, there is a greater quantity of law involved if the bartender is the victim of an injury than if he is the offender. It also would also be expected that the quantity of law would be greater in the preceding examples if the victim and offender were strangers than if they were known to each other.

Finally, Black's theory of law provides some suggestions about the nature of stranger homicide cases for which victim/offender relationships are not recorded. On the face of it, it must be said that Black's theory is not more useful than hypotheses about seriousness suggested by Gottfredson and Hindelang (1979a). Earlier it was suggested that if seriousness determined the behavior of criminal justice processes, why were stranger homicides underreported, since they involved the most serious offense? One may ask the same question of Black's theory: if stranger violence involves a maximizing of law, why are stranger homicides underreported?

There are two answers to the question of underreporting. First, while law is a form of social control, it operates in conjunction with other forms of social control. As was suggested in Chapter 2, homicide investigations involving family members and friends can obtain information from those sources in determining victim/offender relationships. For stranger violence, that network is absent and information is unavailable. What the missing values may indicate is the failure of law when it cannot operate against a background of other forms of social control.

Second, the missing information may reflect that, within the limited resources of police investigation, the information on the victim/offender relationship was not available. In these instances, it is a question of resource allocation that determines which homicide cases are deemed to be important. The latter, in turn, is related to social dimensions and the quantity of law.

In other words, stranger violence is not a homogeneous category. As was suggested above, the quantity of law varies among violent events by strangers according to the rank of the offender and victim, their respectability, degree of organization, and the distance between strangers on these dimensions. The latter leads to the general hypothesis that missing values in homicide cases are those involving a small quantity of law. In other words, the missing information occurs most often for those cases involving confrontational violence rather than robberies or rapes. The latter is consistent with the finding reported in Chapter 2 that 62 percent of those cases with "undetermined motives" probably did not involve robbery (Zimring and Zuehl, 1986). Cases with missing values also probably involve poor or black offenders and victims.

THE FUTURE OF TRUST

One of the most serious aspects of stranger violence is the extent to which it undermines the civil trust that is the central element in routine urban interaction. Despite its essential character, little has been written on the nature of trust in human relationships. The most useful definition has been given by Barber:

> In its most general sense, trust means the expectations, which all humans in society internalize, that the natural order - both physical and biological - and the moral social order will persist and be more or less realized. (Barber, 1983: 9)

Not only does trust refer to a belief that the bridge will not fall and the building is safe, it refers to social expectations that the behavior of others will be orderly, regular, stable, and persistent. For social order to exist at all, others must behave in a trustworthy manner. This is true not only for the deeds of others, but for their words as well. As Bok indicates in discussing truthfulness:

> The function of the principle of veracity as a foundation is evident when we think of trust. I can have   different kinds of trust: that you will treat me fairly, that you will have my interests at heart, that you will do me no harm. But if I do not trust your word, can I have genuine trust in the first three? If there is no confidence in the truthfulness of others, is there any way to assess their fairness, their intentions to help or to harm? How, then, can they be trusted? Whatever matters to human beings, trust is the atmosphere in which it thrives. (Bok, 1978: 33)

Consideration of some of the major ideas presented in this book indicates the critical nature of trust. Selective and spontaneous relationships between strangers assume that there are shared expectations about others that allow for regular and orderly interaction. The taken-for-granted character of stranger interaction refers to those reflexive expectations of regular and persistent behavior.

Stranger violence is similar to terrorism in that, by creating a climate of fear, it undermines the trust that governs our relationships with others. While the intent of terrorists is to create a climate of fear among many people, the intent of stranger violent offenders is to create fear in the victim. Such fear in the victim is, however, cumulative in its effect. Not only the victim, but others who are aware of location as a site for violent victimization avoid it and introduce other changes in their lifestyle. A large part of contemporary urban lifestyles has to do with developing strategies to protect and prevent oneself from being victimized by strangers.

Sometimes, this involves manipulation of time and space to avoid contacts with strangers. These strategies are sufficiently well known that they are part of the information disseminated by groups with an interest in crime prevention education. Thus, groups like the National Safety Council (1972) advise the public to avoid walking on the street at night, walk with another person, never take shortcuts through poorly lit areas, etc.

Protective and preventive measures to avoid stranger victimization are not limited to individuals. Where the target of stranger violence has greater resources, technological devices are added. For example, the efforts of the Southland Corporation, owner of Seven-Eleven Food stores, rely on a variety of spatial, procedural and technological approaches to reduce the attractiveness of their stores as a target for robberies:

1. Cash registers have been made more visible by moving them up front, by lowering window advertising, and by installing exterior lighting. Such efforts make it easier to see in the store from the street.

2. Back door and alley exits have been eliminated. It was found that single exit stores increase the risk of capture and are, therefore, less attractive targets.

3. Special safes, Timed Access Cash Controllers (TACCs), have been installed. TACCs have a two compartment design. One holds a great deal of money securely. The other dispenses only a small amount of money every two minutes. As large bills

come in, clerks deposit them immediately in the TACC's hold compartment. As they need change, they press a button, and the safe's distribution compartment releases $10 in small bills and coins. But after each disbursement, an internal timer prevents another for two minutes. Robbers want to commit the crime as quickly as possible and are not prepared to wait for the safe to dispense the money needed.

4. Southland trains employees how to respond to robbers. The fundamentals are: keep it short and smooth. Never argue. Never attempt any heroics. Just hand over the money and concentrate on getting a good description. (Southern Illinoisan, 1984: 33)

In the short term, such efforts are probably effective. There are, however, characteristics of the use of technology in the prevention of stranger violence that have some long-term negative implications.

The most important characteristics are that protective procedures and technological devices tend to become part of an escalating process between the victim and the offender. McIntosh (1971) shows that the history of safecracking provides an example of how an improvement in protection technology is followed by the successful efforts of safecrackers to render the protection useless. This, in turn, leads to improved technology which is again defeated by the ingenuity of safecrackers.

Since Elizabethan days, strong-box locks with other locks had been vulnerable to the Black Art of skeleton keys and pick-locks. But this was defeated when the warded lock was replaced by the lever or tumbler lock. In turn, techniques were developed for forcing locks off and for defending against this; for drilling holes in locks by various means and for defending against these; for dynamiting locks and defending against this, and so on. The technology of the peter-man (safecracker) has by now moved through gelignite, oxy-acetylene or oxy-arc cutting equipment and even to the use of the thermic lance to cut through concrete to get at a safe, which puts some safe breakers at the fore-front of technological advance. (McIntosh, 1971: 117)

One of the problems with a reliance on technological forms of protection is that they are target specific; they are concerned with reducing the opportunity of violent crime at a specific location. Because they are target specific, they may not result in a general decrease in violent crime, but only result in a change of location and target.

Downtown targets become too well-fortified so offenders attack targets in the suburbs.

In addition, the escalating character of technological protection, whether it is for home or business, creates an increasing cost. The costs of locks are a minor item, but as burglaries and robberies increase, people resort to the more costly alternatives of burglar bars, alarm services, and elaborate security systems.

Because of the target-specific character and because of the increasing costs, the extent of technological protection varies with the victim's ability to pay for it. In a broader context, it means that homes of the wealthy and middle class, as well as business organizations, will be well protected, while the poor will remain vulnerable. Indeed, their vulnerability will increase as well-fortified sites drive offenders in the direction of less affluent, but more vulnerable targets.

The process of escalation in protective procedures and technological devices can continue to lengths that can scarcely be imagined today. It is, however, more likely that technology will increase to the point where the offender's behavior is displaced. Rather than attacking an ever better fortified target, he or she will attack the weak link---the humans manning the system. As McIntosh (1971) and Letkeman (1973) note, there is a tendency to move away from violence toward technological devices to violence toward people.

People become the chink in the armor of technological protection; cash in transit, for example, is more vulnerable than cash kept in a locked place. The professional burglar comes to be replaced by the armed robber thus increasing the risks of injury and death to the victim.

In short, the long-term consequences of an emphasis on technological protection may be to increase the number of violent stranger encounters, particularly those involving selective relationships. Because technological approaches do not address the social causes and effects of such stranger encounters, a continuing erosion of trust can be expected.

The future of trust is not bright. I expect that efforts at crime control will continue to rely on modifications of physical settings in the form of target hardening and increasing use of technological protection. As stranger violent encounters increase, the urban dweller becomes less trustful of his or her fellow citizen, violence becomes more impersonal, and the quality of urban life deteriorates.

The problem is best summed up by a current writer:

> What is at stake here is city life. The words city and civilization have the same root. Cities are not merely the repository of

civilization---the art and the music and the theater---they are marketplaces, crossroads, where all kinds of people come together. That's why young people head for cities. Every advanced industrial society enjoys city life, and in most of the cities citizens take for granted that they can get from their house to the corner in safety. We do not need self-appointed vigilantes, but we do need a system that retires the predators rather than the rest of us. We can survive with plastic ID cards and closed-circuit surveillance, but then we will have lost part of what life is about. (Smith, 1985: 64)

NOTES

1. We take it as axiomatic that official statistics reflect the organizational definition of the event. Thus, official records indicate what is important to the organization and, more importantly in this instance, what is not (Riedel, 1987).

2. Black's definition of stranger relationships is not a residual definition. First, he indicates that strangers represent "positive" relationships in much the same sense as Simmel. The latter are to be distinguished from instances where there is no contact with other groups. Second, Black suggests that the use of law is maximized in stranger relationships and minimized among intimates and those groups where there is no contact.

REFERENCES

Aker, J. R. (1987). Capital punishment by the numbers: An analysis of McCleskey v. Kemp. Criminal Law Bulletin, 23, 454-482.

Barber, B. (1983). The logic and limits of trust. New Brunswick: Rutgers University Press.

Black, D. (1976). The behavior of law. New York: Academic Press.

Black, D. (1979). Common sense in the sociology of law. American Sociological Review, 44, 18-27.

Bok, S. (1978). Lying: Moral choice in public and private life. New York: Random House.

Forst, B., et al. (1981). Arrest convictability as a measure of police performance. Washington, D.C.: Institute for Law and Social Research.

Gottfredson, M. R. & Gottfredson, D. M. (1988). Decision making in criminal justice: Toward the rational exercise of discretion. New York: Plenum Press.

Gottfredson, M. R. & Hindelang, M. J. (1979a). A study of The Behavior of Law. American Sociological Review, 44, 3-18.

Gottfredson, M. R. & Hindelang, M. J. (1979b). Theory and research in the sociology of law. American Sociological Review, 44, 27-37.

Johnson, G. B. (1941). The negro and crime. Annals of the American Academy of Political and Social Science, 271, 93-104.

Letkeman, P. (1973). Crime as work. Englewood Cliffs: Prentice-Hall.

Lofland, L. H. (1973). A world of strangers: Order and action in urban public space. New York: Basic Books.

Lundsgaarde, H. F. (1977). Murder in space city: A culturalanalysis of Houston homicide patterns. New York: Oxford University Press.

McIntosh, M. (1971). Changes in the organization of thieving. In S. Cohen (Ed.), Images of deviance (pp. 98-133). Harmondsworth: Penguin Books.

National Safety Council (1972). Safety on the streets: Manual of safe procedures for women. Chicago: National Safety Council.

Riedel, M. (1987). Official statistics and research on crime, unpublished paper.

Short, J. F. (1985). The level of explanation problem in criminology. In R. F. Meier (Ed.), Theoretical methods in criminology (pp. 51-72). Beverly Hills: Sage Publications.

Smith, A. (1985). The city as the OK corral. Esquire, 62-64.

Southern Illinoisan (12/2/84). 7-Eleven sets example with robbery prevention. 33.

Vera Institute of Justice (1977). Felony arrests: Their prosecution and disposition in New York city's courts. New York: Vera Institute of Justice.

Zimring, F. E. & Zuehl, J. (1986). Victim injury and death in urban robbery: A Chicago study. Journal of Legal Studies, 15, 1-40.